Deborah Price

MONEY
THERAPY

MONEY
THERAPY

Deborah L. Price

Using the Eight Money Types to Create Wealth and Prosperity

Foreword by Sondra Plone, Ph.D.

NEW WORLD LIBRARY
NOVATO, CALIFORNIA

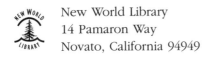

New World Library
14 Pamaron Way
Novato, California 94949

Edited by Georgia Ann Hughes
Front cover design by Mary Ann Casler
Text design and typography by Tona Pearce Myers

Library of Congress Cataloging-in-Publication Data
Price, Deborah L.
  Money therapy : using the eight money types to create
  wealth and prosperity / by Deborah L. Price.
    p. cm.
  ISBN 1-57731-157-4 (cloth)
  1. Finance, Personal — Psychological aspects. 2. Money
  — Psychological aspects. I. Title.
HG179.P7354 2000
332.024'01—dc21   00-056089

First Printing, September 2000
ISBN 1-57731-157-4
Printed in Canada on acid-free paper
Distributed to the trade by Publishers Group West

10 9 8 7 6 5 4 3 2 1

This book is dedicated to my daughter, Anjelica Price-Rocha, for the love, beauty, and wisdom she has brought into my life, and in loving memory of my friend, Barbara Lossos, whose spirit is with us still.

CONTENTS

ACKNOWLEDGMENTS

*I*t took a village to write this book. I am blessed to have an amazing community of friends, family, and colleagues who have encouraged and supported me in my efforts to write this book. With gratitude and thanks, I acknowledge each of you. I would like to specifically acknowledge:

My agent, Sheree Bykofsky, and Janet Rosen for believing in this book in the first place.

My editor, Georgia Hughes and everyone at New World Library for their efforts in making this book possible.

Carol Weser, for being my eyes when I couldn't see.

Charlotte and Rodney Strong, for the gift of my life at Toad Hollow.

My daughter, Anjelica, for her immense patience and understanding.

The Wild Women of Healdsburg for all those Friday nights that saved me.

James Black and Julie Simons, for their care and feeding.

My wonderful friends and family Marge Abrams, Brenda Ferreira, Elizabeth Harlow, Leslie Gainer, Marian Morioka, Mary Rubio, Carol Bell, Molly Light, Benjamin Schick, Caite Mathis, Julie Greenwalt, Kris Cuneo, Randy Price, Stephanie Skidmore, and Bob Rembowski — I love you all.

My mother, Pat Price and my sister, Tricia Davisson for their love and faith in me.

Sandy Plone, for the foreword of this book and for being my dear friend.

My clients who have stood by me and supported me through my life's many changes. I am grateful.

Peace and blessings to every one of you.

FOREWORD

This wonderful book, *Money Therapy*, represents a previously missing tool to help individuals reconstruct their financial lives through the perspective of their spiritual development. Deborah Price has honed her knowledge, beliefs, and concepts into an amazing blend of expertise, in order to guide and educate others toward their highest potential. It is an outstanding contribution to the field, and those who have the courage to read and utilize its wisdom will benefit.

Many authors have written about prosperity — including about how success, power, fame, and money are interrelated with spirituality. As a clinical psychologist, I have learned from my clients' (and my own) struggles and conflicts what a core issue money represents in our psyches, our relationship, and in all aspects of our lives.

My first contact with Deborah Price was as my financial consultant, and subsequently, a dear friend. Her wisdom, dedication to helping her clients, and a level of
integrity that transcended that of most people in the
business world are apparent. She began the task of edu-
cating me about financial matters, gradually guiding me
from "innocence" into accepting responsibility for my
financial life. My journey had been dedicated to helping
others heal childhood wounds and master the complex-
ities of modern life. We both became acutely aware of
the overlap between financial consulting, psychology,
and the spiritual path we shared.

Money seems to represent the ultimate taboo! Many
authors and therapists alike agree that people find it easier to reveal sexual confidences, for example, than to
speak of money matters. Yet the power of early experiences and deeply held beliefs about money is clear.
When individuals explore their treasured myths, conscious or unconscious, it becomes possible to better
understand blocks or patterns that then guide their
financial decisions. Money can be a symbol in families
for love as well as a symbol for violence. It may be used
as a weapon in relationships, manipulating conflicts
about sex, love, or power. Husbands and wives, parents
and children, siblings — we're all prey to the anger,
envy, love, compassion, or worries about money in
these complex relationships.

Having a harmonious relationship with one's
finances is part of the mind/body/spirit connection to
living a balanced and healthy life, and the prosperity
principle is an attitude about life. A consciousness of
abundance can become a self-fulfilling prophecy, as can

a consciousness of scarcity. When clients ask how they might accomplish this shift, I encourage them to find a trustworthy advisor, to read available books on the subject, and to illuminate, understand and then remove destructive myths or childhood beliefs that may block the path to prosperity.

Deborah Price has integrated sound psychological principles and universal spiritual beliefs with her extensive knowledge of financial planning in an easily readable, articulate form. Therapists will be recommending this book to couples as part of premarital counseling to help prevent later conflicts, and to young and mature individuals alike for a journey of self-discovery toward a peaceful and prosperous life.

Sondra Plone, Ph.D.
Clinical Psychologist
Los Angeles, California

INTRODUCTION

*Man is born free; and everywhere
he is in chains.*

— Rousseau, *The Social Contract*, 1762

oday, in the wealthiest country in the world, the symptoms of fear, stress, and anxiety over money permeate our society. They affect both rich and poor and are perhaps the tie that most binds us and makes us more alike than we realize. Although the symptoms are different for each person, almost everyone suffers from one form or another of the "condition." While many drugs are available to help us manage other fear and anxiety disorders, one has yet to be invented to cure us of our money problems.

It has always been my nature to observe. I have spent hundreds of hours and countless days of my life just sitting and watching the human drama play out before me. I love life and people immensely and have always held great hope in my heart for humanity. In the last few years, however, what I have seen has alarmed and disturbed me so profoundly that it has become increasingly difficult to remain a silent witness of what I see unfolding before me.

In my work as a financial consultant, I have also seen disturbing behavior in people struggling away to acquire more and more material possessions, with an ever-increasing sense of hopelessness and financial despair. People come to me seeking "financial security" and searching for something more meaningful in their lives. Unfortunately, far too often, "more" means a new car, a boat, a bigger house, some *thing,* which only serves to increase their burden and further complicate their lives. Repeatedly, I have watched people become enslaved by their insatiable need for more things, so much so that their life's energy becomes depleted. I do not make this statement with any judgment. Rather, I make it because I believe that we have been living in a consumer coma for too long and that the consequences of this mass unconsciousness greatly affect our psyches and are reflected in the devastated world around us. We have become so numb to the reality of what is *really* happening that we have become too immobilized to take any action and to make the changes necessary to sustain our lives on this planet.

Advertising and the media have convinced us that we are nothing without money and material possessions. We are in the grips of a national obsession. We have been brainwashed into believing this "stuff" is what we're supposed to want, that fulfillment comes from what we have rather than from how we live and feel. At a time when we are running out of space to build more shopping malls, the Internet has created a virtual shopping mall that will allow us to shop twenty-four hours a day in a quest to fill the void we deeply feel but fail to understand. Meanwhile, the billions of dollars spent exploiting our mass addiction for buying things we don't really need could be used to save the Earth as it teeters on the edge of the precipice.

Consumerism is the addiction of our time, and it is time we owned up to it, because we have far too much to lose. I wrote *Money Therapy* to help you remember the purpose of your life: the original purpose. The one you were born to live. You were not born to shop. You were not born to live your life indebted to the things you own. You were not meant to spend your life's energy working so that you could simply accumulate material possessions. That is not what prosperity and abundance are about. Money is a tool meant to help transform your life in more meaningful ways. As a tool, it will help facilitate the path of true fulfillment that comes from living your life intentionally and with purpose. It does not matter how much money you have if all you are doing is spending it to accumulate more things. This kind of spending is a waste of your life's currency. You were meant for far greater things, and within you resides a far greater truth. It is this truth that I seek to help you rediscover. You have the power within you to manifest all that you desire. You also have the power to evolve and to choose to make a difference. We must all wake up and become part of the solution. For it is entirely possible that we are playing the final round of the money game called "all or nothing." Waking up is not easy, but in my experience, when we fail to hear the alarm, we are often rudely awakened by whatever means it takes to get our attention.

MY WAKE-UP CALL

Six years ago, the world as I knew it literally fell apart. On January 17, 1994, the Northridge earthquake hit Los Angeles. I had a premonition that it was coming. The day before I had an architect friend come to visit me, and I asked him to evaluate the apartment building I was living in to see if it would hold up to a major earthquake. He humored me and checked out the building, saying it looked pretty sound and that it should hold up quite well. At approximately 4:00 the next morning, the earthquake hit. I was already awake. It felt and sounded like a bomb had hit us. I ran across the hall to grab my baby girl in the darkness and chaos. A few minutes later another earthquake hit, and we could hear the building beginning to split at the seams. My husband and I, fearing for our lives, decided to get out of our third-floor apartment. We found our way to the front door only to discover we were locked in. It was pitch black, electric sparks hissed and flew around the room, and the smell of gas began to fill the air. I crawled on my hands and knees in the dark, frantically searching for my keys. As I waded through the glass and debris, my mind was flooded with fearful thoughts. Was this the end? Would we survive? My keys were nowhere to be found. I was not ready to die. As I thought of my baby, I grew determined to find a way out. Then, out of the corner of my eye, I saw the glimmer of my keys lying in a heap of rubble. They were easily two hundred feet from the table I had placed them on. I crawled back to the front door and unlocked it, and we ran down the stairs to our neighbors. Together, with our children in tow, we drove down Montana Avenue, one of the wealthiest neighborhoods in the world, which now looked like a war zone. The sky was an eerie greenish black. All the signals had stopped working, and the streetlights had gone out. Slowly, we caravanned down the road, following our friends to the shelter of their parent's home, where we sat through what was the coldest, darkest night of my life. Huddled together in the living room, we cried and waited, wondering what the world would look like in the dawn.

Three days after the earthquake, I packed up my family and left Los Angeles to rebuild my life. Both my home and business were condemned. There was little left to salvage. I never went back to the apartment. I couldn't bear to see it again. Few of my friends or family could understand how I could leave my entire life behind without even knowing where I was going. It was okay that I did not know. I knew the earthquake was my wake-up call, intended to shake me out of the life I had been living and to discover the life I was meant to live. I had received enough signs and messages to know I was not where I was supposed to be; I had been unhappy with life in the city for years. The smog, the traffic, the crime were all beginning to get to me. I longed for a simpler life. When my daughter was born, my desire to escape the city grew even stronger. After the earthquake, I could no longer go home or go to work. Since home and work were gone anyway, I knew it was time to surrender to God's plan. When we left, I only knew I was supposed to head north and have faith. The rest would be revealed to me in time.

Now, years later, I believe that the earthquake, although a terrifying experience, was a blessing in disguise. I did not lose anything that could not be recovered or that I could not live without. Even after the earthquake, I experienced many more losses, more "aftershocks." I now see this part of my life as a long phase of learning to let go. The more I let go, the more room I had for what I truly needed and the more receptive I became to living my life's purpose.

Today, I live in the country surrounded by nature and tranquility. In the stillness of this space, my mind was allowed to become quiet, and for the first time since I was a child, I could hear the voice within me and all that it needed to say. I have learned that everything that falls apart comes together again. Our lives are like great mosaics. When we take the time to piece them together and to stand back and look at them, we see that every piece fits perfectly and beautifully together. The same is true of your life. This book will help you examine the pieces of your life differently. It will help you to become clearer about who you are and what you truly value. When you create the mosaic of your life, money should be part of the frame, not the picture.

EXPLORING OUR RELATIONSHIP TO MONEY

Money possesses an energy and life of its own. It contains a duality similar to that present in our own nature. It is both spiritual and material, creative and destructive, loving and cruel. It can help us to fulfill our greatest dreams or it can lead us to be defeated by our worst nightmares. Our relationship to money is perhaps God's grandest experiment with the children of his invention. For we have given money such power that it permeates every part of our existence. It is more than a means of exchange; it has become our "other" life. And all too often, it is the life we pay the greatest attention and tribute to, at the expense of experiencing the richness that lies within our unexplored potential.

Our unconscious and unhealthy relationships with money have caused many of the problems we experience both individually and collectively. One of the ways to explore how these unconscious relationships work is by identifying and observing your primary money archetype. An archetype consists of unconscious patterns, thoughts, or beliefs that are active in your life. In chapter 3, you will discover how your particular archetype has influenced your relationship with money. Learning to identify and work with your money archetype requires looking into the mirror of your soul. The money archetype that is active at this moment in your life is the place you have been asked to grow. As we change and become increasingly conscious, we often move from one archetypal phase to another. This movement is a necessary part of the journey, which ultimately, in our most conscious phase, that of the money Magician, renders us truly enlightened. It is only then that we realize that by honoring the self, we honor the Spirit. As a reward for our courage to take this inner journey, we become transformed by our knowledge and realize our power to manifest whatever we desire. When we arrive at this place, we see ourselves as we never have before. The face staring back at us in the mirror is no longer a stranger in a strange land, but the image of our true self.

WHY I WROTE THIS BOOK

The purpose of this book is to help you explore the great mystery of money so that you may find your own path. This journey is about truth, self-discovery, and enlightenment. It will challenge your belief system about money. It will build the bridge between the past and the present so that you may learn to master your future. It will shake you from the deep sleep of unconsciousness. You will awaken to see yourself for the first time, as the Magician you were meant to be, who knows not only where the source of money lies, but who holds the key to unlocking its door.

I wrote this book to help you find the key to who you really are and what you are truly seeking. There are as many paths as there are travelers. Follow the path that led you to pick up this book. What are you seeking? What do you want to change? Let the answers to these questions be your starting point. I highly recommend that you keep a Money Therapy journal to record your responses to the exercises throughout the book. Most of my clients have benefited greatly from the insights gained by keeping a journal. It is also a great way to track your progress.

As you move through this book, you may wish to skim some chapters or skip them altogether. That's okay. It may be that you've already traveled that road and know its landscape well. Or perhaps you will revisit a chapter later that you are not quite ready to explore now. However, resist the temptation to take a shortcut simply because it appears the easier way to get to your destination. Taking the easiest route often results in unnecessary detours or roadblocks to your success. Wherever your destination may lie, use your heart as a guide and Spirit as your compass, and you will surely find your way.

Chapter 1

THE MONEY GAME

*Man must choose whether to be rich in things
or in the freedom to use them.*

— Ivan Illich, *Deschooling Society,* 1971

*I*n my work as a financial consultant during the
past fifteen years, I have frequently observed the game
people play with money. The primary objective of this game
is to hide and keep hidden the deep layer of anxiety, fear,
and shame we feel about money. Silently, we have lived
with this discomfort, accepting it as our fate. We have
become skillful players at this game of hide-and-seek, but
we have forgotten that what lies hidden still lives within
us. We have become disconnected from our inner reality,
thus giving away our power and leaving little room for
understanding our relationship with money and its meaning in our lives. Having relinquished control, we have
become the pawns in the money game and let money rule
our every move.

Unconsciously, we have accepted that money is our greatest resource, and then we feel we have wasted, neglected, abused, avoided, or coveted it. You name it, most of us have done it. Secretly, we feel guilty and ashamed and unable to communicate these feelings to others. How did we as a civilization come to not only surrender our power to money but also deny the control it has over our lives and well-being?

Many civilizations existed before us that never used a currency or even knew what money was. When money finally came into use, it began to shape history and our belief system in profound and lasting ways. Even centuries later, we do not understand all the effects of money on our lives or how it shapes our world. Money's meaning continues to elude us. Today, because of the inconceivable power and emphasis we have given it, the money game dictates our daily lives. We make decisions based on our feelings of not having enough money, we change careers because we want more money, and many even marry or divorce because of money. Practically every major decision we make is somehow shaped or influenced by money. Yet rarely do we examine what we're truly seeking. Never before has humankind created a game so widely played that has no rule book, guidelines, or training. It is no wonder we hide. We don't even know the rules!

SOME ESSENTIAL TRUTHS ABOUT MONEY

How did money became so powerful, when, in fact, it consists of pieces of paper that only have value to the extent that we believe they do? We have not understood that money, quite literally, is worth *nothing* without our belief in it. We created it. We gave it value. We made it powerful. And then, as the money game grew, these pieces of paper became our greatest resource, a resource so valuable that many people unconsciously worship it above all else. Now, our greatest misfortune is that without money, we feel that we are nothing.

Money is both mysterious and elusive. The more we are defined by it, struggle to get it, and greatly need it, the harder it is to obtain. One of the most amazing keys to having more money is to surrender to it. We must learn to integrate the universal spiritual laws into the world of money; the greatest of these laws is to surrender to what we cannot control.

We cannot and do not control money. Money is a commodity. Its value changes not only in relation to the economy but also in relation to our consciousness. We cannot control money, but by understanding it, we can obtain what we need. Money is not a part of us. We can never truly own it, because it isn't really ours. And to the extent that we maintain the illusion of money as our safety net, we will remain prisoners of our own making. *Money will own us if we let it.*

DEFINING THE MONEY GAME

Our currency states the truth in its four simple words printed across each bill: "In God We Trust." It might as well say, "In Money, Our God, We Trust." That would be more honest. That would let us off the hook a bit by stating openly that money is what we truly believe in. Whether or not we are conscious of it, this truth is woven into the very fabric of our existence. We have put our faith and trust in money. This is one of the unspoken rules of the game. Few of us possess the insight to recognize this basic paradox. We have been programmed to believe in the material and the tangible. As a result, no matter how much money we have or how many possessions we accumulate, we do not experience fulfillment, and our endless search for substitutes to fill the void continues. Looking deeper into the symbolism found on our dollar, we find many other subliminal messages. First, our money is green, a color that symbolizes growth and resources. On the front of the dollar is a picture of our founding father, symbolizing the leadership of money as patriarchal. In our society, money has a distinctly male energy and is equated with winning and success. The largest money game in the world, Wall Street, is still largely controlled by men, with women representing less than 12 percent of that population. (This patriarchy, however, does not extend to having money. While markets are dominated by men, over half of this country's wealth belongs to women.)

In today's world, the "Wall Street" money game stands at the top of the hierarchy and is the game everyone wants to play. However, the deck is loaded and the stakes are high, since we don't have access to the rule book.

Money has even more hidden meanings. When you turn the dollar bill over, you find the two great American seals: one, the American eagle, which is largely familiar, and the other, written in Latin, which is not widely understood. This more obscure seal is quite telling: inside it is a pyramid, consisting of thirteen stones, representing the original thirteen colonies. An "enlightened eye" stands at the top of the pyramid. The words above the all-seeing, all-knowing eye, *annuit cœptis,* are taken from Virgil and mean "He, God has smiled on our endeavor." At the bottom of the pyramid are the words *novus ordo seclorum,* which translate as "the new order of the ages," also adapted from Virgil. For a country founded on the principle of separation of church and state, there certainly are plenty of references to God on our money!

All evidence suggests that money, God, and religion were intertwined from the beginning of civilization. So it is no small wonder that money has become such a powerful force. Beneath all the symbolism is another hidden message that cuts to the core of the money game: If you're good and you play by the rules, we, the gatekeepers, will show you the way to this powerful resource. In fact, the creation of the dollar was the birth of the first pyramid scheme, more popularly referred to as capitalism.

MONEY UNCONSCIOUSNESS AS THE ROOT OF OUR PAIN

Capitalism and its underlying drive toward consumerism greatly influence the financial infrastructure of our own lives and how we deal with money. Perhaps our need for money is as much about sustaining our way of life and the survival of capitalism as it is about feeding our own unconscious needs and desires.

At any rate, of this I am certain: Money plays far too great a role in our lives for us to remain unconscious of what it means to us as individuals. We must become aware of its impact on our lives and our choices. Continuing to play the money game and denying that we live in the thrall of money only perpetuates our fears and anxieties, chipping away at our souls. As stated by philosopher Jacob Needleman in his book *Money and the Meaning of Life:*

"Money enters so deeply into our personality and into our psychophysical organism that the personal exploration of money is necessary for the discovery of oneself, the discovery of those hidden parts of human nature…that need to be in relationship to our consciousness."[1]

Our lack of attention to our relationship with money is undoubtedly the root of much of our pain. It has often saddened me to witness the shame people experience over money. In conversations with my clients, I have discovered that much of our money shame comes from feeling like we don't handle it well, that we're "bad" with money. Each of us needs to carefully reexamine what path we are taking toward fulfillment. Fulfillment is not about filling your life up with material possessions. Yes, I know the thrill of spending money can feel like an "E" ticket at Disneyland. But when the ride is over, it's over. That is pleasure, not fulfillment, and it wears off. The quick-fix approach will never cure us; it merely masks our deeper desire for meaning.

SEARCHING FOR MEANING IN THE MATERIAL WORLD

When I was twenty-nine years old, not long after my divorce, I started to experience an unfamiliar restlessness. Although my marriage had failed, I was in a new relationship that was loving and fulfilling. My business was beginning to take off. I was making more money than I'd ever made before. I was the master of my own destiny, and yet I felt oddly detached from my life. I remember saying to myself, Okay, you've done all this, now what?

---

[1] Jacob Needleman, *Money and the Meaning of Life* (New York: Doubleday, 1991), p. 206.

Then one day, as I was driving to work, I suddenly made a left turn and found myself sitting in the parking lot of a Porsche dealership. I had never even thought of buying a Porsche. Stunned, I sat for a while in my old but perfectly fine Mercedes-Benz, wondering to myself, What in the hell am I doing here? I truly didn't know. Finally a salesman approached my car and asked if he could help me. I looked him directly in the eye and said, "Yes, I came to buy a Porsche, but I have to do it quickly because I've got to get back to my office." He chuckled, but said he'd do his best to accommodate my schedule.

Two hours later, I drove out of that dealership in a brand-new midnight blue 944 Porsche coupe, fully equipped. I couldn't really afford it, but that salesman just happened to be the owner of the dealership. After talking with me, he thought the car was just what I needed. So, he cosigned for it, telling me if I was ever late on one payment he would personally come and take it back.

How to Know What Is Real in Your Life

For a while that car brought me a great deal of pleasure. I felt successful. People thought I was successful. Some even thought I was rich. It was an enlightening experience. I was the same person I always was. All that had happened was that I had purchased an expensive sports car, a status symbol (and one usually owned by men), and it had changed my life. I was perceived and treated differently, and not always for the better. People were envious, and my car was vandalized several times. One time, someone carved their feelings about my car into its sides with a key. I also began to attract people who were more materialistic than I was comfortable with. The Porsche never really mattered much to me. It was a fun toy, but I didn't really identify with it. Getting the car did not cure my restlessness. It did, however, motivate me to work harder so that I could keep up with the payments.

My experience with that car forced me to look more closely at what I valued. I had everything I had ever wanted. My problem was, I didn't believe that it was real. Subconsciously, I was looking for some external way to make my success more tangible, and I manifested the car as proof. It did not work. It took a good therapist and doing my own spiritual work to finally learn what was real.

What I learned, and what I hope to impart to you, is that only one thing is real: your connection to Spirit, however you define it, and your faith in that Spirit. There is no other security. Without this connection, we will never feel that we are loved enough, that we have enough, that we *are* enough. Without this faith, we will not know true fulfillment, regardless of how much money we have or how many things we try to fill our lives with.

UNDERSTANDING THE ENERGY OF MONEY

Do not misunderstand me. I am not saying that money is bad, because it isn't. I happen to like money: I'm just not attached to it. It is just something that happens to have a lot of energy. If you use it consciously, the energy of money can manifest whatever you desire in your life. Conversely, when you use the energy of money unconsciously, it can draw things into your life that you could not possibly anticipate or desire.

It took me a long time to reach this understanding. It is no accident that I wrote this book or that Money Therapy is my teaching. I have spent a great deal of my life learning about money. I have chased money, made money, married money, loved money, and hated money. I have experienced the thrill of having it all and the agony of losing it. Put simply, playing the money game can be quite costly. It is the ultimate game of "truth or consequences," in which we learn that without the truth, we are left to live in the shadow of self-deception latent with unknown consequences.

WHY WE LOSE THE MONEY GAME

When it comes to money, most people lead imagined as opposed to real lives. We imagine what our lives will be when we're "rich." We imagine the great deeds we can do, the difference we can make. We imagine what we could have, buy, or become. We measure the possibility of our greatness according to the amount of wealth bestowed upon us. We have been fantasizing instead of living and becoming what we desire. In the process, we have become disconnected from our innate power to manifest our own reality.

We have given our power away to money. In effect, we're telling ourselves: "I can't do it on my own, it's too hard, I'm too tired. Here, you do it for me." If the money shows up in our lives, we can be and have what we imagined. If it doesn't, then we cannot. Living this way, we do not have to be responsible for what happens in our lives. After all, we were not in charge of our money. The money didn't show up; therefore, little of who or what we dreamed of happened either.

At the other end of the money spectrum lies a different kind of player. These players have already "made it" and are considered by most standards "rich." It matters not whether they earned the money, won it, inherited it, or stole it: The result is the same. We think that the end — lots of money — justifies the means. Most of us believe that having money will buy us freedom and unlimited options. This isn't true. In my experience, people with money suffer as much as those without; it is just a different kind of suffering, as evidenced by the hordes of the newly rich in the Silicon Valley who are flocking to therapists to treat their "sudden wealth syndrome."

Having all the freedom and options in the world can be a terrible burden to even the most well-adjusted person, and this is even more true if you do not have your act together. Wealth does not suddenly make personal or psychological problems disappear. To the contrary, it often magnifies them. Having that much power can work against you — or the people in your life — if you're not careful how you use it. Unfortunately, since most of us still carry around a fair amount of unresolved baggage, having money only adds to our load. It's not as if you can just go out and buy a new set of empty baggage. We have to carry that old stuff around. Only now, our baggage is heavier. It has money in it, lots of money.

People with money play the money game in different ways. They don't have to imagine their lives the way others do. Instead, they feel a need to do something with their lives and with all that money. They have to watch over it, invest it wisely, give it away to the "right" causes, decide how to spend it, and accumulate more. This process creates a tremendous cautiousness; you can't be too careful when you have money. You have to have your guard up, because suddenly it's hard to know whom you can trust. Even J. Paul Getty, one of the richest men in the world, once said, "I find having all this money a considerable burden."

People with money often feel guilty and undeserving. Having money frequently causes relationship problems, especially if one person has significantly more than the other. People with money often have difficulty with trust and intimacy; they are often envied by their closest friends and family members and are pursued by the greed of others. Observing this cautiousness and difficulty with intimacy in my clients and others caused me to conclude that it is impossible to be truly free if you are constantly feeling the need to be guarded and have difficulty knowing whom or what you can trust. Consequently, wealth without consciousness is but another state of poverty. This kind of poverty is often overlooked, because it is invisible on the outside. If we could see inside these people, however, we would see as much fear and loneliness as exists in any state of poverty, only we seldom empathize with the rich.

A New Way to Win the Money Game

We have set ourselves up to lose the money game. Fortunately, we can learn to play it differently. This book will offer you some new strategies for success that can lead you to greater abundance and a sense of fulfillment — the kind of fulfillment that comes from within. The process of Money Therapy will help you discover your own truth about money and its meaning in your life. Part of this process is to look at how we arrived where we are, both personally and historically, and then to explore ways to move beyond this place.

The eight money types, described in chapter 3, can become a guide to discovering the impact of your past experiences with money and to changing your approach in the future. You will learn to identify unconscious beliefs and behavior patterns that may be obstacles to receiving all that is available to you. Recognizing your money type is key to understanding the meaning behind why you hide and what you are truly seeking.

As you proceed through this book and work through the exercises, you will begin to peel back the layers of your unconscious. As you become more aware of how you play the money game, you can begin to identify the obstacles in your path and discover ways to make meaningful change. It is only through increasing your awareness that you can change your relationship with money and begin to play the money game differently. It is time to create your own rules based on your own truth. When you do, you will have reclaimed your power and you will begin to manifest the world you truly desire.

We need to stop giving away our power and to learn that the source of money, and of all things, exists within each of us. The most effective and powerful way to tap into this source is through our daily connection to Spirit. Throughout this book you will be asked to look inward, to find your own source. You will learn to harness the power within you. In achieving this, you will hold the key to manifesting your own reality — including money.

EXERCISE

Grand Scale Imagining

♦♦♦♦♦♦♦♦♦♦♦♦♦♦♦♦♦♦♦♦♦♦♦♦♦♦♦♦♦♦♦♦♦♦♦♦

This exercise is designed to help you become clear about your real values. It will help you to define what having money really means to you. It will provide a new framework for understanding the relationship between your money and your life. It is important to always remember what it is you are truly seeking. When what you seek is grounded in your own truth, you are infinitely powerful in your ability to transform your reality.

You have just received news that you have won the lottery. Your entire life, as you have known it, is about to change forever. Complete the following exercise, answering the questions as honestly as you can.

I suggest you begin using your Money Therapy journal with this exercise. The process of recording your responses in a journal will help you track your progress and will provide you with valuable insight about yourself.

1. How much is your lottery ticket worth?
2. How does having all that money make you feel?
3. How much money per month do you plan to give yourself to live on?

4. In what way (or ways) will the quality of your life be affected?
5. Do you have any fears about how this money might change you or your life?
6. If given a choice, would you prefer that people know or not know of your newly acquired wealth?
7. What are you going to do with the money? Make a specific plan. Write it down step-by-step.
8. What aspects of your plan are essential to your happiness?

Write these aspects of your plan on a separate sheet of paper. Carry this around with you, in your purse or wallet. Read it daily. Meditate or pray for guidance in helping you manifest it. Believe in it so that you may become it.

Chapter 2

OLD GAMES

Knowledge of the universal origins builds the bridge between the lost and abandoned world of the past and the still largely inconceivable world of the future. How should we lay hold of the future, how should we assimilate it, unless we are in possession of the human experience which the past has bequeathed us?

— Carl Jung, "The Gifted Child," 1943

Exploring our historical relationship with money, both as influenced by the very distant past and by our own experience, is essential to understanding and changing our relationship with it. History has played a significant role in forming the unconscious patterns and beliefs that shape our lives and decisions. Carl Jung, the founder of analytic psychology, helped us to understand that the entire human experience is stored in the "collective unconscious" and is manifested in our lives through archetypes. Jung believed that archetypes were collectively inherited unconscious patterns of thought, ideas, and images that exist in our individual psyches. These archetypes, and the collective unconscious, affect our actions, motives, and behavior.

Today the relationship we have with money consists of more than just our personal experience. It also includes another layer of reality that predates our individual lives. Although this reality remains an unconscious mystery to most of us, we are nonetheless affected by it. To the extent that you can lift the veil between the collective unconscious and your conscious reality, you will be able to understand and change your relationship with money and its meaning in your life. To simplify this concept, imagine that you are a computer with two separate databases. One of these databases was already stored on your hard drive when you were born. This database represents the collective unconscious. The other database consists of the life experiences you have had from birth until this minute; it holds both your conscious and unconscious history.

One of the things that separate us from other living things and make us human is our ability to become conscious and, through that consciousness, to alter our reality. With the guidance offered in this chapter, you will be able to retrieve the information that has been stored in your unconscious and explore its significance in your life today. Before we can change where we are going, however, we must first understand where we have been. Although we are powerless to rewrite history, we are infinitely powerful, through knowledge and creativity, to reinvent the future.

Money has preoccupied us and influenced our actions for centuries. For more than three thousand years, money has manifested in many forms, from seashells, cacao beans, and slabs of stone to various gold and silver coins stamped with images of gods and leaders. Yet, in spite of its long history, money remains a subject that is neither taught nor widely understood. If the purpose of history is to understand where we came from so that we may apply those lessons to our future, it seems rather remarkable that money as a topic of history has been swept under the proverbial rug. Have we chosen to disregard the history of money because it is far too frightening to look at? Or have our attempts to understand it, let alone explain it, simply failed? Regardless of the reasons for this avoidance, it remains clear that we must develop a basic understanding of our historical experience if we are to shift our individual and collective consciousness about money.

THE ABBREVIATED HISTORY OF MONEY

Just as there have been times of great economic prosperity when civilizations grew to unparalleled heights, there have also been periods when money and its use have disappeared completely for hundreds of years. Money has repeatedly disappeared and resurfaced during humankind's ongoing attempt to financially control our destiny and that of the world.

From the beginning of recorded history, human beings exchanged goods and services as a means of survival. Commodities such as food, animals, fur, tobacco, and even people, in the form of slavery, have been exchanged for the goods and services of others. This exchange of one thing for another, however, had a very different energy from the exchange of money for goods. Early commerce created community by necessity. People had little choice but to rely on one another for basic needs and survival. Money altered this reality and

changed human experience in ways that were inconceivable before its invention. As people began to rely on
one another less and less, the experience of community
became diminished, although we still long for it. Once
money was in widespread use, the needs and desires of
human beings changed dramatically, and they have
grown more complex and challenging ever since.

THE BIRTH OF MONEY

Although money in the form of gold and silver ingots
(referred to by the ancient Hebrews as shekels) were
used as far back as end of the third millennium B.C. in
Mesopotamia, precious metals were too scarce for any
widespread trade or economy to be possible. The real
birth of money, virtually changing the course of human
history, came between 560 and 546 B.C. when Croesus,
the king of Lydia, began making the first standardized
gold and silver coins for the purpose of commerce. This
new medium of exchange gave rise to the first retail marketplace, giving people far greater access to goods and
services than they had ever had before. As money,
goods, and commerce increased, so did the human desire
for more. It is interesting to note that the Lydians not only
invented coins but also the dice, forging a relationship
between money and gambling that lives on today.

In his efforts to conquer other kingdoms and
because of general conspicuous consumption, in a relatively short period of time, the wealth created by
Croesus was all but spent. Although the Lydian Empire
fell, the money legacy the Lydians left behind would
shape the world in ways that no one could have previously imagined.

As neighbors of Lydia, the Greeks were aware of the Lydians' success with coins and commerce. Coincidentally, the Greeks had also just discovered silver deposits near Athens. Before long, the Greeks began minting silver coins, and Greece became the center of trade for the eastern Mediterranean world. As the trade business grew, it brought a tremendous source of wealth.

Money not only changed the way business was conducted in Greece, it also changed the relationship between people and money. Along with changing Greece's social structure, the widespread use of money also extended Greece's ties to the outside world. As a result, relationships that were once based on established connections and survival no longer bound people together. As money changed the relationships between people and the world around them, it also changed their values and beliefs. As wealth grew, people began to have more leisure time and to pursue new forms of artistic and intellectual endeavors. For the first time, because of the influence of money, the creative human potential could be taken to new heights. In ancient Greece, money gave rise to intellectual, artistic, and spiritual transformation.

MONEY AND GREED: EARLY WARNING SIGNS

News of coin money eventually traveled to Rome. In no time at all, the Romans began minting their own coins and building the first money-centric civilization in the world. Although the Greeks used money, the Romans created the first global marketplace and were also the first consumer-oriented society. Quick to discover how money could buy them almost anything, the Romans

went on a spending binge that would ultimately destroy
them. (The phrase "shop till you drop" was probably
first used during this era!) Rather than becoming pro-
ducers themselves, the Romans relied heavily on the outside world. When they ran short of money, they simply
financed large armies to plunder the riches from others
lands. Between the ever-rising military cost and their
insatiable and extravagant lifestyle, the Romans finally
hit bottom by the end of the fourth century with the fall
of Rome. This great money-centered society managed to
survive for nearly a century, only to fall beneath the
weight of its own greed. Instead of facing their own
responsibility (as is true of all addicts), the Romans
blamed money for being the source of their demise. The
fall of the Roman Empire was followed by the period
known as the Dark Ages, and money, the convenient
scapegoat, all but disappeared from Western Europe for
nearly one thousand years.

PLANTING THE SEEDS OF MISTRUST

By the beginning of the twelfth century, Europeans
had developed such a mistrust of money that even the
wealthy did not want to associate directly with it. The
Crusaders solved this dilemma by creating a sacred military order known as the Knights of the Temple of
Solomon in Jerusalem. The Templars, as they were
known, were chaste and spiritually devout; they were
also fierce warriors with sworn vows to protect the Holy
Land and the riches of the European nobility. The
Templars created a powerful international banking insti-
tution by providing financial transactions and protection
on behalf of the rich for a fee. They were highly revered,

and by all accounts the trust they received was truly earned by their commitment and loyalty to their vows.

At this same time, the King of France, Phillipe II, was running short on funds. Phillipe the Fair, as he was known, was ruthless and vain and had an insatiable appetite. He was a tyrant of the worst kind. Knowing that the Templars had possession of the greatest source of wealth, he set his sights on attaining it. Because he knew how beloved the Templars were, he knew he could not wage war against them, so he set out on a path of merciless persecution. By accusing them of sexual perversion, human sacrifice, sodomy, and cannibalism, King Phillipe convinced his people that the Templars had obtained their wealth through making a pact with the devil. Subsequently, in 1310, the Templars were publicly tortured into confessions and burned at the stake. In the aftermath, the Christians lost the Holy Land to the Muslims. This story, as well as the story of Sodom and Gomorrah in the Bible, has been interpreted as a sign of God's wrath over the sins of the people.

After the demise of the Templars, the battle between church and state over who would control their fortune began in earnest. Within a year, due to severe financial abuses of the king, another financial empire had collapsed, and both the pope and the king of France were dead, leaving yet another lasting impression on the collective psyches of humankind.

THE FIRST GOLD RUSH

Shortly after Columbus "discovered" the Americas, the Spanish and Portuguese kings began to mine the riches of native Indians throughout North and South America. Their hungry pursuit of gold and silver brought a great influx of money to all corners of the world. This pursuit unleashed a force that could not be contained.

Between 1500 and 1800, the Spanish and Portuguese had brought literally tons of silver and gold into circulation. Unfortunately, the Spanish and Portuguese royalty did not heed the lessons of their European neighbors. They consumed heavily, and they also could not get enough. So much money flooded their economies that a wave of inflation began that could not be stopped. There was so much gold and silver that the rich lined everything in it, from their buildings to their clothing, wearing their wealth as a symbol of power and status. Although money continued to pour in, the kings spent it faster than it could be shipped. Eventually, they were forced to borrow from other governments, who did not hesitate to charge them a high premium for their expensive lifestyles. Jack Weatherford best describes the force of money created during this time in his book *The History of Money:*

> In conquering America, Spain opened a pipeline that pumped a torrent of silver into the world's economy, but Spain was helpless to control that flow. Neither Chinese emperor nor Ottoman sultan, neither the Persian shah nor Russian czar proved any more adept at channeling or controlling it than the Spanish kings. Spain had unleashed a power that raced around the globe and operated with a force of its own,

independent of church and state. The wealth of America had run amok, and the world would never again be the same.[1]

THE LAST FRONTIER: MONEY IN AMERICA

Although paper money was invented by the Chinese as far back as the first century A.D., its widespread use was pioneered in the United States by Benjamin Franklin, who clearly envisioned the role that paper money would play in modern economic life. Benjamin Franklin was a deeply spiritual man who valued ideas above money and a staunch advocate of hard work and moderate consumption. (If only Ben could see us now!) By the end of the American Revolution, which was largely financed by paper money, the United States was heavily in debt. American currency had become so devalued that it was practically worthless. In 1780, Congress stopped issuing paper currency. The public distrust of paper money became so great that paper currency remained absent for nearly a century.

As we well know, however, paper money was resurrected by the first Legal Tender Act in 1862 and continued to be backed by the gold standard until 1971. With economic problems and a war that needed financing, President Richard Nixon recognized that he needed more money than could be backed by the government or its gold reserves. As a result, Nixon convinced Congress to take the U.S. dollar off the gold standard

---

[1] Jack Weatherford, *The History of Money* (New York: Three Rivers Press, 1997), p. 108.

altogether. Following in the footsteps of previous rulers throughout history, Nixon was given free rein to borrow billions of dollars to finance the government's needs.

Today the U.S dollar is a fiat currency, which means that it is created by and made legal by our government and is not based on or convertible to anything. Although the U.S. government owns over $100 billion in gold reserves, none of these reserves provides any security against the U.S. dollar. The money we use is backed by nothing more than our belief in it and our government's ability to control it. Since our money was no longer redeemable in gold, new money was printed and the inscription *Payable to the Bearer on Demand* was replaced with the words *In God We Trust.*

Thus, the leaders of our country created the first money system based purely on belief rather than on tangible reality. The words *In God We Trust* stand as a lasting testimony to the fact that our leaders had no idea what the consequences of this choice would be. The fate of our world and of money was placed in the hands of God. Whether our leaders knew it or not, this move placed us closer to the truth about money than ever before.

MONEY AND ITS MEANING TODAY

Thousands of years and untold experiences have passed, and still the subject of money and its meaning remain unconscious mysteries to most of us. It is time for that to state to change. Historically, when the movement of money begins to expand and reshape itself, the existing financial and social infrastructure has always changed. Today technology has created the fastest, most illusive form of money ever known or imagined. The gold harvested in the Silicon Valley has unleashed yet another powerful influx of money that is flooding the world.

Electronic money flows through invisible currents across the globe with the click of a mouse. Never before has so much wealth had the capacity to move so quickly and to change the fate of so many people in a matter of seconds. We have created such a powerful force, and yet we still fail to understand its greater meaning and relationship to our lives. This lack of consciousness has not served us well historically. If we could create the reality of the world around us without money consciousness, imagine what we could do *with* money consciousness!

The ability to change and manifest your reality moves in direct relationship to your level of consciousness. If you desire your relationship with money to change, you need to be willing to look at how you arrived where you are today. As your awareness grows, you can consciously begin on the path to where you want to be. You will realize your own power to manifest whatever you desire. But first you must travel the journey within to uncover the deeper meaning of money and its purpose in your life.

As a metaphor, money represents the duality of our nature as human beings. It is no accident that there are two sides to every coin and dollar bill. One side represents our individual and collective ability to master the material world. The other, of equal importance, represents our ability to master the spiritual dimension, the inner world. It is this resource that we have left untapped. Until we turn the coin over and explore the spiritual dimension of money and the opportunity it presents for enlightenment, money will always be elusive. Seeking to possess it without understanding its true purpose and meaning will only leave us feeling more conflicted and unfulfilled. Until we understand its true meaning, we will remain enslaved by money and the material world. We will have traveled far, only to arrive at our destination having left the gift at the altar. The real journey is not about money: It is about you. It is an archeological dig to the center of the truth of who you really are and what your path and purpose are. The closer you get to the truth, the closer you are to the source of the invisible supply, which is limitless and available to us all.

THE NEW AGE OF MONEY

Although we have become increasingly clever at manipulating and even creating new forms of money, we still have much to learn. Our collective history may help us to understand the unconscious origins of fear and distrust that surround our relationship with money, but it only presents part of the picture. We must also carefully examine and understand our individual histories and personal experiences with money. In the next chapter, you will learn about how the various "money types" relate to money and you will be able to identify and explore your primary money type. These money types, like archetypes, are based on subconscious patterns that evolved out of your own history. Some of this history contains inherited patterns of thought, ideas, and images that have been passed down through the collective unconscious.

By exploring your money type, you can learn how it has played out in the drama of your life.

We all have a story. Some of us have bigger stories than others. Some of us are more attached to our stories than others and are committed to maintaining our part in the script as our legacy. Others feel ashamed or embarrassed by their histories and feel uncomfortable with sharing it. Whatever your personal experience and history of money is, your story must be told so that you can then witness it objectively and consciously. The following exercise is intended to help you explore and observe your relationship to money in the context of your personal history. In the process, you will discover how your money type has manifested certain beliefs and behavior in your relationship with money.

Use your journal to record your answers to the following questions:

1. What is your earliest memory of money?
2. How old were you. What was the experience?
3. How did that experience affect you?

Now, using the answers to these questions as the starting point, write your money biography. Include as many details as you can remember: what happened, how old you were, how you felt. Who are the key people in your biography, and what messages, patterns, or behavior related to money did you receive or inherit from them?

Once you've finished with your money biography, ask yourself the following questions:

1. What does your personal history reveal about your relationship with money today?
2. What values, beliefs, or judgments about money are related to your personal experience and/or family history?
3. Which of these values, beliefs, or judgments are active in your life today?
4. Are they working for you or against you?
5. Is this where you want to be with money? If not, where would you rather be?

Chapter 3

THE EIGHT MONEY TYPES

*It is our less conscious thoughts and our less conscious
actions which mainly mould our lives and the lives
of those who spring from us.*

— Samuel Butler, *The Way of All Flesh*, 1903

I think it is safe to say that most people harbor
unresolved money issues. These unresolved feeling or experiences in turn create patterns of behavior
that are often self-limiting and self-defeating. Looking
beyond the surface of money to consider how you make
financial decisions can prove to be one of the best steps
you can take toward improving your relationship with
money. Money Therapy can help you explore the inner
life of money. It can provide a framework for uncover-
ing your unconscious motivations and behavior related
to money. In my work, I have discovered eight basic
ways in which people react to and handle money. These
types represent eight patterns people follow, and by
understanding your type, you will discover the reasons

behind previous conflicts or issues you have had with money. This becomes the first step to reaching your personal financial goals. Once you discover your type, you can use Money Therapy to work toward becoming a money Magician, the eighth money type, the one we all want to work toward becoming.

Many people do extensive financial planning, only to repeatedly make the same mistakes or to never implement any plan at all. Those clients who are willing to explore the inner life of money are much more likely to reach their financial goals. They have an easier time making financial decisions and are more successful at manifesting money and realizing their dreams. Clearly, there is a direct connection between having a healthier, more conscious relationship with money and creating prosperity.

It takes time and patience to learn to become a money Magician. The first step is to look into yourself for the answers. You must know why you want to be a money Magician before you can become one. As I have observed people over the years, I've noticed eight basic ways in which they relate to money. The eight money types are repeated patterns of behavior that reside in your unconscious. By discovering and evaluating your particular money type, you can begin a different kind of financial education that is specific to you, one that is almost absent today in the financial world. Money Therapy provides the framework on which each individual's response and resulting "picture" are filled in, according to their unique background, beliefs, and experience. Doing this work will make you better prepared to realize your long-term goals.

THE EIGHT MONEY TYPES

Most people fall into one or more of the eight money types. Much like Jungian archetypes or the Enneagram, which defines different personality types, this system offers a simple way to identify and assess your relationship with money. With this understanding, you will learn how to make conscious choices, and, as a result, the money dynamic at work in your daily life will improve.

In this book I refer to the eight basic money types as the "players" in the money game. Although we may be successful in most areas of our lives, when faced with money decisions, changes, or crises many people revert to an ineffective, emotional approach to making decisions about money. By beginning to understand your underlying unconscious feelings and beliefs about money, you will become better prepared and more conscious of the patterns and issues as they surface in your life. Following are descriptions of the eight money types.

The Innocent

The Innocent takes the ostrich approach to money matters. Innocents often live in denial, burying their heads in the sand so they won't have to see what is going on around them. The Innocent is easily overwhelmed by financial information and relies heavily on the advice and opinions of others. Innocents are perhaps the most trusting of all the money types because they do not see people or situations for what they are. They are not unlike small children in the sense that they have not yet learned to judge or discern others' motives or behavior. While this trait can be very endearing, it is also precarious for an adult trying to cope in the real world. We all start out our journey in life as Innocents. However, as we grow and develop, the veil of innocence is lifted and replaced by our experience with the outer world.

Characteristics of the Innocent Type	
Trusting	Financially dependent
Indecisive	Nonconfrontational
Happy-go-lucky (externally)	Feels powerless
Fearful or anxious (internally)	Represses feelings and beliefs
	Seeks security

The Innocent's goal is safety at all costs. The primary fear is abandonment. I have encountered far more female Innocents than male, although both exist. That so many women are Innocents is most likely due to their cultural training to be unassertive and trusting. The Innocent is often romantically paired with Tyrant or Warrior money types, who both thrive on rescuing the Innocent.

The lesson for the Innocent is to claim her own power and to learn to find safety in the knowledge of her own capabilities. By allowing herself to experience her independence, her fear of abandonment will dissipate, as will her innocence. In time she will become fully capable of experiencing her own power. The Innocent is like Dorothy in *The Wizard of Oz*. She must learn that not even the wizard can take her home; she must discover the power within herself. Once she does, she can find her way anywhere.

The Victim

Victims are prone to living in the past and blaming their financial woes on external factors. Passive-aggressive (prone to acting out their feelings in passive ways rather than through direct action) in nature, Victims often appear disguised as Innocents, because they seem so powerless and appear to want others to take care of them. However, this appearance is often either a conscious or subconscious ploy to get others to do for them what they refuse to do for themselves. Victims generally have a litany of excuses for why they are not more successful, and they are all based on their historical mythology. That is not to say that bad things haven't actually happened to Victims. More often than not, Victims have been abused, betrayed, or have suffered some great loss. The problem is that they have never processed their pain, and so it has turned on them. Victims are always looking for someone to rescue them, because they believe they have suffered enough. They carry a sense of entitlement: "I paid my dues, look at my battle scars, where's my due?"

Characteristics of the Victim Type	
Prone to blaming others	Resentful
Highly emotional	Unforgiving
(melancholy or angry)	Addictive
Lives in the past	Lives out a self-fulfilling
Financially irresponsible	prophecy
Seeks to be rescued	Feels powerless

For the Victims' paradigm to shift, Victims must learn to understand and heal their past wounds. Of all the money types I have worked with, Victims hold onto the key to unlocking the door of their potential the tightest. It's almost as if at some point Victims decided that their history was much more interesting and exciting than any future they might have. As a result, they formed a lifetime attachment to living out the drama of their pasts. After all, when you are the star, producer, and director of your own lifelong soap opera, it can become pretty hard to let go of those roles. It feels risky: There might not be a role like it ever again.

The Victim's primary fear is of being betrayed. Ironically, what Victims do not see is that they are most often betrayed by themselves. Spiritual transformation for Victims comes when they are able to see how using their past experiences can act as a powerful tool and catalyst for change. When Victims have taken the journey inward and healed the wounds of the past, they are prepared to move fully into life. Until they do, they are not truly living in the present and certainly have little promise of a future. They are simply living off the reruns, which inevitably become pretty monotonous, no matter how good the story was. Moving out of this drama is deeply profound for the Victim. Because the Victim generally has truly suffered, when she becomes enlightened, she brings forth a great capacity for compassion, love, and understanding, qualities essential in the making of all great Magicians.

One of the most dramatic transformation stories I have ever witnessed involved my client Janet, who was a classic Victim. She came to me desiring to "get her financial act together." She was very smart, had a good job, and was constantly getting into financial difficulty. When we talked about her childhood and her family experiences with money, it became clear that she was repeating an old pattern. Her family was lower middle class and had struggled financially her entire life. She felt that their lack of money and inability to support her financially had kept her from becoming what she always dreamt of being: a lawyer. She managed to work her way through college, but that was it. When her father died, she felt like she needed to work to help her mother, who still had two children at home. As a result, Janet felt betrayed and let down. She complained about always having to do everything for herself and not being able to rely on anyone. Emotionally, she was very angry at and resentful of the people in her life. Financially, she had gotten herself into heavy debt, had fallen behind on her bills, and was plagued by creditors. She had been married twice, and during both marriages she felt she hadn't really been taken care of. I told her I could help her only if she agreed to go into therapy, because otherwise she would end up right back in the same boat. Tired of her circumstances, she did. A year later, and after a lot of work, Janet's life completely changed. In therapy she learned to address her anger and feelings of having been betrayed and began to see how those feeling prevented her from taking responsibility for herself. She had been playing the same tape over and over in her mind for so long that it had become her mantra: "If I'd only been born richer, if my parents had helped me more, if the men in my life really loved me...." As we began to do Money Therapy, Janet began to integrate what she had learned in therapy with how the Victim dynamic manifested itself in her financial life. What she learned was that she had become overly invested in being financially unsuccessful. Her lack of success was proof of how she had been robbed of her life's opportunities. Her feelings of betrayal were so deep that she wore them like a badge of honor. The state of her financial affairs was a symbol of how everything had been taken from her. As her awareness grew, she began to wake up and take responsibility. The young woman who had once had big dreams and had managed to put herself through college was intelligent, strong, and capable.

Once we work through our anger and resentment, we pass into the light and truth of who we are. Our essence is who we are, not what happened to us. But first we must see it before we can be it. Janet did not become a lawyer, and she realized later that being a lawyer was not really her destiny. She did, however, become a highly compensated personal coach who helps take both corporations and individuals to their next level of achievement by helping them recognize their obstacles. She serves as a wonderful example of a money Magician who goes on not only to teach what transformed her, but also to turn that enlightenment into money, the physical manifestation of the lesson.

The Warrior

The Warrior sets out to conquer the money world and is generally seen as successful in the business and financial worlds. Warriors are adept investors — focused, decisive, and in control. Although Warriors will listen to advisors, they make their own decisions and rely on their own instincts and resources to guide them.

Warriors often have difficulty recognizing the difference between what appears to be an adversary and a worthy opponent. A worthy opponent should be embraced as an opportunity to put down the sword and recognize the potential for growth and transformation being offered in disguise. Worthy opponents are most easily recognized as the person with whom you have the greatest conflict. When we are willing to step back and recognize the lesson and truth this person has to teach, even when it is disguised as conflict, their presence is worthy of our attention. When we recognize the conflict as an opportunity for growth, our "opponent" has, in fact, served us. The world is filled with Warrior types, who run the gamut from enjoying the sport of business and the skillful art of negotiating to those whose single-minded intent is simply to win at any cost.

Characteristics of the Warrior Type	
Powerful	Confident
Driven	Calculating
Loyal	Generous
Competitive	Rescuer
Disciplined	Wise
Goal oriented	Discerning
Financially successful	

The primary fears at the heart of a Warrior are dependence and loss of power. The spiritual journey of Warriors, financially speaking, is to understand what it is they are truly seeking to protect or conquer and to establish boundaries around what is truly important to them. This means knowing when to pick up the sword and why and when to put it down. We all need a bit of healthy Warrior inside of us. It is this dimension of us that makes things happen. The question is, at what cost? An enlightened Warrior knows the answer.

Throughout a large part of my life, both as a child and an adult, I was ruled by the Warrior. I was well liked because I was fun, loyal, protective, and trustworthy (common traits in young Warriors). However, I was a fighter and responded fiercely to any act of injustice imposed on myself or others, which created a lot of conflict in my life. I remember my sister asking once, "Why do you always fight back? If you'd just shut up, you wouldn't get into so much trouble." But I was a leader, and I wanted to be in control. Over time my behavior proved to be a bit isolating, because as I matured I recognized that I intimidated people, even adults. In doing my own work, I began to realize that I was pretty heavily armored and that I was the person whom I most sought to protect. Financially, I was always tripping uphill and could never ask for help. Warriors don't ask for help because they fear that would mean they are weak or in need. Most people would rather not do verbal battle with a Warrior. They tend to be razor sharp, quick, and to know all your weak points.

In my mid-twenties, I realized I was having a spiritual crisis. An avid reader, I always sought solace in a good book. I was drawn to Shatki Gawain's book *Living in the Light,* which opened my eyes and led me to seek the help of a psychologist. I knew there were parts of myself that I did not see clearly or understand. In my first session, I told my therapist that I knew I needed new skills and understanding before I could move beyond my history and alter the path of my future. Together we embarked upon a journey of discovery that changed my life forever.

Not only did I learn to put down my sword, but I

learned why I had carried it so long and so close to my heart. It was both a psychological and spiritual journey. On the other side, there really is a light. It is you, the soul within you, which is the way God shines through you.

The Martyr

Martyrs are so busy taking care of others' needs that they often neglect their own. Financially speaking, Martyrs generally do more for others than they do for themselves. They often rescue others (a child, spouse, friend, partner) from some circumstance or other. However, Martyrs give with attachment and are repeatedly let down when others fail to meet up to their expectations. They have formed an unconscious attachment to their own suffering.

The Martyr moves between two distinctly different energies: one that seeks to be in control and is controlling of others and the other being the wounded, often very needy, child. Martyrs tend to be perfectionists and have high expectations of themselves and of others, which makes them quite capable of realizing their dreams because they put so much energy into needing to be right. Like Victims, Martyrs often live in high drama, experience a lot of highs and lows, and struggle with their attachment to negative experience. They see the glass as half empty instead of half full. Their focus on the negative often keeps them from realizing the deep wisdom that lies within their experience. Martyrs who are willing to do their own work to heal their woundedness have the capacity to become gifted healers and powerful manifestors — money Magicians. (The story on page 79 is a good example of a Martyr.)

Characteristics of the Martyr Type	
Controlling	Critical and judgmental
Manipulative	Perfectionist
Long-suffering	Resentful
Secretive	Passive-aggressive
Caretaker	Compassionate
Self-sacrificing	Wise
Disappointed	

The Fool

The Fool plays by a different set of rules altogether. A gambler by nature, the Fool is always looking for a windfall of money by taking financial shortcuts. Even though the familiar adage "a fool and his money are soon parted" often comes true, Fools often win because they are willing to throw the dice; they are willing to take chances. The Fool is really a combination of the Innocent and the Warrior. Like the Innocent, the Fool often has impaired judgment and has difficulty seeing the truth about things. An adventurer, the Fool gets caught up in the enthusiasm of the moment, caring little for the details. The primary difference between Fools and Innocents is that Fools are relatively fearless in their endeavors and remain eternal optimists regardless of the circumstances. In this manner, Fools are like Warriors in that they seem to always land on their feet and are not easily defeated. The Fool also sets out to conquer the world but is easily distracted and lacks the discipline of the Warrior. The Fool is much more interested in making money as a sport or form of recreation than as a serious endeavor. Fools would happily give the shirt off their backs only to realize later that it wasn't their shirt or that it was their last.

The Fool does possess some rather remarkable qualities that if mastered make her quite capable of becoming a Magician. The Fool lives very much in the moment and is quite unattached to future outcome. Most of what Fools pursue is for the simple pleasure of doing it. Most of us could learn from this characteristic of the Fool. However, until the Fool becomes enlightened, he will continue to attract money easily, only to have it quickly slip through his fingers because he's simply not paying attention.

Characteristics of the Fool Type	
Restless	Overly generous
Undisciplined	Happy-go-lucky
Financially irresponsible	Adventurous
Impetuous	Lives for today
Optimistic	

The Creator/Artist

Creators/Artists are on a spiritual or artistic path. They often find living in the material world difficult and frequently have a conflicted love/hate relationship with money. They love money for the freedom it buys them but have little or no desire to participate in the material world. The Creator/Artist often overly identifies with the interior world and may even despise those who live in the material world. Their negative beliefs about materialism only create a block to the very key to the freedom they so desire. Creators/Artists most fear being inauthentic or not being true to themselves.

Since it is almost impossible to attract what we are repelled by, the Creator/Artist is constantly struggling for financial survival. This is not because they lack talent or ambition. Rather, they are stuck in a belief system that disempowers their ability to manifest money. Too many people on the creative or artistic path feel that money is bad or lacking in spirituality. This is only true to the extent that one believes it is true. And to the extent that Creators/Artists maintain this belief system, they are limiting themselves and creating a block to the flow of money.

The Creators/Artists who work to integrate the spiritual with the material world will find an end to their struggles. Since they have often spent much of their time and paid much attention to their inner journeys and creative potential, Creators/Artists already possess many of the qualities necessary to become Magicians. This type most needs to accept the world they live in and embrace its many dimensions. To stop suffering from the tension we feel between the spiritual and material worlds, we must learn to embrace both worlds as part of our own duality.

Characteristics of the Creator/Artist Type

Highly artistic and/or spiritual	Detached Nonmaterialistic
Passive	Loner
Internally motivated	Seeker of truth

I have worked extensively with creative people and feel a special affinity with them. While I recognize that it can be difficult to live in a world that does not value spirituality or creativity as much as other fields, it simply does not serve us to resent that reality. Doing so only serves to widen the distance between the spiritual and the material rather than encouraging us to find ways to bridge the gap. My friends and clients who have managed to straddle both worlds are among the most successful and happiest people I know.

Several years ago I encouraged one of my clients, Ray, to stop putting price tags on his paintings. I asked him to consider letting people offer to pay what they wanted or could afford to pay. I asked him to consider surrendering to the process, to just do his work and to ask God and the universe to support him in his efforts and to be specific about what he needed. Intuitively I knew he was too attached to receiving a high amount for his work as proof that he was valued. This attachment was causing a constriction in him that was blocking the flow of money. His work was wonderful, but his self-esteem was low. Although Ray was very evolved spiritually and artistically, he was missing a significant piece of the puzzle. It is no easy task to recognize our own resistance as the next point of transformation.

My advice was initially not well received. Ray felt strongly that he had the right to ask a certain price for his paintings, and that was that. I let it go. About a year after we had this discussion, Ray called to inform me that he was leaving to live in Europe. He said, "I finally took your advice, and I've sold almost everything. I have enough money to go to Europe for a year or two, and when I run out, I'll come back." That was in 1995, and Ray has yet to return. Periodically, I get a postcard and a glimpse of him living the life he always wanted to live, free of any self-imposed restrictions. In helping Ray to surrender his attachment to the way money shows up, I was able to become the sacred witness of its mysterious flow to someone expressing his truth and living in faith.

The Tyrant

Tyrants use money to control people, events, and circumstances. The Tyrant hoards money, using it to manipulate and control others. Although Tyrants may have everything they need or desire, they never feel complete, comfortable, or at peace. The Tyrant's greatest fear is loss of control. Tyrants are often overdeveloped Warriors who have become highly invested in their need for control and dominance. While Warriors are often heroic in their true concern for others' welfare, Tyrants are purely self-interested. This type is interested in power and control for their own sake and will forsake other people if necessary to gain more of it. Throughout history, the Tyrant has emerged as the ruler who dominates and destroys with no sign of remorse. Today Tyrants are the political leaders, business people, or family figureheads who use whatever means necessary to win at all costs. The Tyrant is a master manipulator of both people and money. Perhaps it's because the Tyrant type is often the most financially successful image we have in our society that so many of us secretly believe that money is bad. Television and the media do their part to further convince us that although we may think we want more money, we just need to look at what's become of those who actually have it. It's enough to make anyone hesitate.

Tyrants, however, are not as rich as they appear. Sure, they have everything money can buy (which often does include beautiful people) and never have to worry about paying the phone bill, but they lack many things that money cannot buy. They are often, in spite of their apparent success, very fearful and rarely feel any sense of fulfillment. The Tyrant suffers from a condition I call "chronic-not-enoughness."

Characteristics of the Tyrant Type	
Controlling	Critical and judgmental
Rigid	Aggressive
Manipulative	Unforgiving
Fearful	Secretive
Oppressive	Highly materialistic
Prone to rage or violence	

The Magician

The Magician is the ideal money type. Using a new and ever-changing set of dynamics both in the material world and in the world of the Spirit, Magicians know how to transform and manifest their own financial reality. At our best, when we are willing to claim our own power, we are all Magicians. The archetype that is active in your life now is the place you need to grow from. By understanding your own personal mythology and the history behind your current money type, you will become conscious of patterns and behavior that are preventing you from having the relationship with money you desire. When you have reached the point of understanding and have become aware of all that you need to know at this point on your journey, you will be ready to transform your newly acquired consciousness into the reality of your life.

The Magician is fully awake and aware of herself and the world around her. The Magician is armed with the knowledge of the past, has made peace with his personal history, and understands that his source of power exists within in his ability to see and live the truth of who he is. Magicians know the source of power to manifest lies in their ability to tap into their Higher Power. With faith, love, and patience, the Magician simply waits in certainty with the knowledge that all our needs are met all the time. Magicians embrace the inner life as the place of spiritual wealth and the outer life as the expression of enlightenment in the material world. They are infinitely connected.

Characteristics of the Magician Type

Spiritual	Powerful
Wise	Optimistic
Conscious	Confident
Vibrant	Compassionate
Trusting	Detached
Generous	Open to flow
Loving	Financially balanced
Fluid	Transforms reality
Lives in the present	Tells the truth

Identifying Your Money Type

◆◆◆◆◆◆◆◆◆◆◆◆◆◆◆◆◆◆◆◆◆◆◆◆◆◆◆◆◆◆◆

Step 1: Now that you have read about the eight money types, you have probably identified with one — or more — of them. Sometimes people have more than one type, which is generally, an indication that you are moving from one phase to another. It's possible that you have some of the characteristics of each type. However, one is usually dominant. To identify your primary type(s), go through the list of characteristics on page 57 and check or circle all the characteristics that apply to you, without thinking about which characteristics relate to which type. As you proceed with this exercise try to view each characteristic in the context of how you react to, relate with, and feel about money and how it affects the relationships in your life. For example, you may be a very generous person in some areas of your life but known to be a bit tight about money.

Step 2: In your journal, write down all the characteristics that you have checked on this list. The chart on page 58 lists all the characteristics with a number beside each. This number represents the type or types each characteristic is associated with.

1 = Innocent
2 = Victim
3 = Warrior
4 = Martyr
5 = Fool
6 = Creator/Artist
7 = Tyrant
8 = Magician

Add up the number of characteristics you have in each category. The category that you have the most number of is your primary money type. If you have more than four in any other category, this is an indication that you have work to complete with this type as well. In the next chapter, we will begin to explore how to change the dynamic of your types by exploring their origins and the opportunity they offer you for transformation.

List of Characteristics

Anxious	Vibrant
Prone to blaming others	Rescuer
Highly emotional	Aggressive
Lives in past	Generous
Financially irresponsible	Loving
Seeks to be rescued	Conscious
Trusting	Open to flow
Feels powerless	Manipulative
Unforgiving	Happy-go-lucky
Addictive	Discerning
Self-sacrificing	Controlling
Resentful	Long-suffering
Passive-aggressive	Caretaker
Compassionate	Financially balanced
Wise	Passive
Restless	Seeks security
Undisciplined	Financially dependent
Fearful	Represses feelings and beliefs
Financially successful	Nonconfrontational
Impetuous	Artistic
Optimistic	Competitive
Overly generous	Prone to rage or violence
Transforms reality	Calculating
Lives for today	Critical and judgmental
Lives out a self-fulfilling prophecy	Secretive
	Adventurous
Powerful	Lives in present
Driven	Internally motivated
Disciplined	Detached
Goal oriented	Highly materialistic
Confident	Indecisive
Loner	Rigid
Seeker of truth	Loyal
Tells the truth	Spiritual
Nonmaterialistic	Oppressive

Key to the Money Type Exercise

Anxious	1	Vibrant	8
Prone to blaming others	2	Rescuer	3
Highly emotional	2	Aggressive	7
Lives in past	2	Generous	3, 8
Financially irresponsible	2, 5	Loving	8
Seeks to be rescued	2	Conscious	8
Trusting	1, 8	Open to flow	8
Feels powerless	1, 2	Manipulative	4, 7
Unforgiving	2, 7	Happy-go-lucky	1, 5
Addictive	2	Discerning	3
Self-sacrificing	4	Controlling	4, 7
Resentful	2, 4	Long-suffering	4
Passive-aggressive	4	Caretaker	4
Compassionate	4, 8	Financially balanced	8
Wise	3, 4, 8	Passive	6
Restless	5	Seeks security	1
Undisciplined	5	Financially dependent	1
Fearful	1, 7	Represses feelings and beliefs	1
Financially successful	3	Nonconfrontational	1
Impetuous	5	Artistic	6
Optimistic	5, 8	Competitive	3
Overly generous	5	Prone to rage or violence	7
Transforms reality	8	Calculating	3
Lives for today	5	Critical and judgmental	4, 7
Lives out a self-fulfilling		Secretive	4, 7
prophecy	2	Adventurous	5
Powerful	3, 8	Lives in present	8
Driven	3	Internally motivated	6
Disciplined	3	Detached	6, 8
Goal oriented	3	Highly materialistic	7
Confident	3, 8	Indecisive	1
Loner	6	Rigid	7
Seeker of truth	6	Loyal	3
Tells the truth	8	Spiritual	6, 8
Nonmaterialistic	6	Oppressive	7

Chapter 4

REDEFINING YOUR
TRUE NET WORTH

*What we must decide is perhaps how we are
valuable rather than how valuable we are.*

— Edgar Z. Friedenberg,
The Vanishing Adolescent, 1959

e live in a culture where the terms *net worth* and
self-worth have become synonymous. Yet they
have entirely different meanings. I have always been
interested in examining language and words for their hidden meanings. Often, if we look closely enough, a far
greater truth lies within words than we had imagined. For
example, if we separate and dissect the words *net* and
worth, an entirely different picture comes into view.

According to *Webster's New Collegiate Dictionary,* the
two most common definitions of the word *net* are 1) anything that catches or traps; ensnares or 2) a net amount,
profit, price, or result; after all considerations; final. The
word *worth* means "monetary" or the "value of something
measured by its qualities or by the esteem in which it is

held." The word *self* means "one's own person as distinct from all others."

Upon considering these words, we discover that most of us have been "trapped and measured" by money, leaving the self rather alone and unaccounted for. Since we often do not feel good about our net worth, our self-worth has become devalued and our self-esteem deflated. This is because we have not properly appreciated ourselves for being intrinsically valuable in our uniqueness, separate from our net worth.

Over the years I have asked hundreds of people to do net worth statements (their financial assets minus their financial liabilities), and without fail, it is the most difficult task to get people to complete. Many clients simply have refused to do one. Others have only done one if I did it with them. Those who have willingly completed the task were few and far between. This resistance was so prevalent that I began to realize that it was not the task, but the emotional turmoil it caused that was at the root of the problem.

When it comes to our net worth, most of us feel that we never quite measure up. Thinking about how much we have accumulated as proof of our value is a painful experience. In our culture, our wealth is the ultimate measure of who we are. We have become defined by it. Those who have little net worth feel a corresponding lack of self-worth. But they are not alone. Many of my clients who have a high net worth also experience similar feelings of low self-esteem. The difference is that although they have plenty of money, they often do not feel worthy of it. They appear to have everything, and yet they feel they are nothing.

I believe this lack of self-esteem is caused by a profound spiritual bankruptcy that is so prevalent in our culture. Having lived a life in pursuit of money and material gain, we have often neglected the self and its inherent longing for spiritual connection. As human beings, we alone have this need. I do not believe this need is simply evolution at work. Rather, it was intended that we value and nurture this dimension of our self above and beyond all else. Without this connection to the self, our true worth is diminished, and life becomes an endless search for substitutes to fill the void.

We have become ensnared in the net, caught in the money trap. I cannot help but believe that we will not escape until we begin to value ourselves above money and material gain. We need to create a new paradigm for living, one that is different from the one we have inherited and maintained for generations out of habit and lack of consciousness.

MORE MONEY MAY NOT BE THE RIGHT ANSWER

We live burdened by thoughts of lack and limitation. We have not been taught to think beyond our historic point of view. Yet we are so much more than simply the sum total of our experiences. There is a truth in each of us that is deeper than any biography of our lives could ever tell. Yes, we are greatly influenced by our backgrounds and experiences, but defining ourselves merely by those is much too limiting.

The story of Ellen, one of my clients, is a good example of this point. As a child and young adult, Ellen was poor and lived in constant fear. She came from a violent, dysfunctional family, and survival was a core

issue for her on many levels. But survive she did. She
went on to become successful in almost every way.
Money and success flowed into her life in great abundance. She was not, however, a happy person. When
Ellen first came to see me, she was severely depressed
and in therapy. We talked specifically about her money
issues. She told me that she needed money to feel safe
but that it caused her difficulty in her relationships.
Actually, it had destroyed every relationship she had
ever had.

Attractive, intelligent, and rich, Ellen easily attracted
men. The problem was that over the years Ellen had
built a fortress around herself, and no one ever really got
in. She was not able to trust anyone enough to be truly
intimate. With her therapist's help, she was able to work
through her feelings about the abuse she suffered as a
child and the pain and anger she felt toward her parents.
However, the money issues continued to interfere in her
relationships. There was still something she needed to
understand that was getting in the way of her happiness.

As we looked at Ellen's past and tried to pull
together the pieces, we found that the only time she
could ever remember feeling safe was right after her
father brought home a paycheck. Because for a while,
when there was money, her family was happy, and the
abuse would stop. Although Ellen had forgotten this, the
memory embedded in her subconscious was played out
in her daily life. Ellen spent most of her time working
and knew she was a workaholic, but she always said it
was because she liked her work. Her workaholism was
one of the major problems in her relationships. The
other was that although Ellen had a lot of money, she

was frugal beyond belief. She didn't enjoy spending her money, and she wasn't good at sharing it. Ellen was a mixture of the Warrior and Tyrant money types.

In looking at her relationships, Ellen began to see how she had pushed the men in her life away even though they had truly loved her. Although neither of the men she had married had as much money as she did, they were successful in their own right. That was the other missing link. Since she was more successful than they and money was her safety net, subconsciously she could not stop working so hard because in her mind her husbands weren't financially reliable. They might not bring in that paycheck, and then what would happen? That left everything up to her, and subconsciously she felt betrayed, and so she sabotaged her relationships.

After about a year of our meetings, Ellen began to see that in working so hard to create her safety net of money, she had never really looked at who she was and what made her happy. She had neglected her self. She always loved art but never considered doing it. She loved children but never had them. There was never time for that. Then one day she called me and said she needed to see me right away. That afternoon Ellen came in and said, "Well, I did it. I've solved my money problems. I gave all my money away."

At first I was disturbed, but as we talked I realized that she had made a good decision. She knew exactly what she was doing. She told me, "Money was my safety net, my protector. But it also kept me from living my life. I had to cut down the net so that I could be free." For Ellen, the net also served as a barrier that kept her from becoming more of who she was. Today Ellen lives on a modest income, paints in her spare time, and works with children. Perhaps most important, she has time to be in touch with her self, with who she really is. She has a real life now and is at peace with her past.

The possibility and potential of each of us are far greater than the sum of our past experiences. Ellen had lived most of her life enmeshed in her history. Although she had succeeded financially, she was not experiencing prosperity on a personal, emotional, or spiritual level. We have to move beyond our personal histories to see our true value and worth.

YOUR MONEY IS NOT YOUR LIFE

It is no wonder that we suffer such lack of self-esteem. Our life's "balance sheets" (financially speaking), if we're brave enough to examine them, often look pretty bleak. Meanwhile, we feel continually pressed to answer questions like, "What do you have to show for your life?" "What does your financial picture look like?" "What are you doing to secure your financial future?" These are not questions that most of us really want to address.

I have a friend who is one of the most capable, intelligent people I know. He runs two businesses, is involved in the community, and is well liked by just about everyone. Recently he attended one of my Money Therapy seminars and told me afterward that he felt deeply ashamed about his finances. When I asked him why, he spilled out a story of how, many years before I knew him, he and his wife had major financial problems and had had to claim bankruptcy. He said, "Every day I think about all the people I never paid back, and every day I worry that it might happen again." I told him that bankruptcy is a choice that deeply affects people's self-esteem, because in the eyes of the world, suddenly you are nothing, you have nothing, you have failed. But that is not the truth about who you are. You are a perfect human being, but that does not mean you don't have problems or won't make mistakes. Bankruptcy is about forgiving debt and letting people start over. But you have to be willing to forgive yourself. You have to be willing to let go and move on, which my friend had been unable to do. Instead of starting over, he carried his shame with him, and it became a far greater burden than any debt he'd ever owed. I offered to help my friend further, but he could not face the depth of his shame. His net worth and self-worth had both become bankrupt, because he could not see his true value, the value of his self.

MONEY THERAPY LIFE INVENTORY

Since dealing with our financial histories and money in general can be so difficult, I developed an "accounting" system that has helped to make the process more positive and pleasant for my clients. I call this system doing a "life inventory," and I have my clients do two types of accounting. One is a traditional process involving a financial review of assets and liabilities; the other is an accounting of one's life. I have come to the conclusion that doing an accounting of one and not the other is unkind and unjust to us as human beings — not to mention the fact that I can actually get people to do some accounting this way and to have fun with it.

Investment professionals are famous for lecturing their clients on the time value of money. This concept basically means that while you have the time, you had better make good use of what money you have (also referred to as the value of compounded dollars). For example, if you are thirty-five years old and want to retire at age sixty-five, you have thirty years to use the money you make today grow into your retirement tomorrow. If you don't take advantage of the time you have now, you will need to save more money, take greater financial risks, or wait longer to retire.

While this is a very valid financial concept, and entirely worth consideration from a logical, financial standpoint, it is not the only perspective. The other truth we need to consider above and beyond our financial net worth is what I call the "time value of life." Unlike money, which we can always find ways to make more of, our life bank only has so many hours in it…and we don't get the privilege of knowing just how many hours we have left. Consequently, we need to consider the value of our life's currency and how well we are spending it before anything else, including money, can have any meaning at all. If all we do is focus on money — making it, spending it, and saving it for the future — we take the very real risk of running out of time. Without this understanding, we will always live in a state of poverty that no amount of money can save us from.

Perhaps if we had a currency with denominations of time printed on it that we actually had to physically spend as we use time, we might value time as much as we value money. Then we would consciously have to spend time dollars with every purchase. We would be compelled to first ask ourselves, "How many life hours am I going to have to spend paying for this? Do I really want or need it that much? How much of my life am I going to consume by my lifestyle?" Or more important, is your "style" robbing you of your life? These are questions we greatly need to ask ourselves in our search for understanding our true worth.

EXERCISE

Your Net Worth

◆◆◆◆◆◆◆◆◆◆◆◆◆◆◆◆◆◆◆◆◆◆◆◆◆◆◆◆◆◆◆◆◆

In determining your true net worth, first you need to conduct an inventory of your life bank. Answer the following questions:

1. How old are you?
2. How many life hours have you spent? (Formula: Twenty-four hours a day x 365 days a year x number of years/days you have lived. For example, on your fortieth birthday you will have spent 350,400 life hours.)
3. How have you spent your time?

Now do an accounting of how you have "spent" your life. Account for everything that is meaningful to you. When you are done, write a list of all the things you still need to do with your life dollars, things that would fulfill you as a human being. Finally, how many life hours a day are you spending toward meeting this goal? If you feel brave, go ahead and do a financial net worth statement too. It's not only a good exercise, but it will give you some useful perspective on how you've used your time versus your money.

If you can't quite muster the courage to do an actual financial statement, at the very least ask yourself the following questions:

1. How many hours a day do you work?
2. How much money do you make per day (average)?
3. How much money do you need to live on per month?
4. How many life hours does it take to make that much money?
5. How much money have you saved?
6. How much money do you owe?
7. How many life hours will it take you to pay it off?
8. How much life does that leave you with?
9. Is your lifestyle worth it?

Brenda is a client of mine who began Money Therapy as an Innocent and gradually became a Warrior. She is now well on her way to becoming a money Magician. She is a forty-three-year-old entrepreneur, artist, and dancer. This excerpt was taken from her Money Therapy journal and is followed by her answers to the above questions.

I am at a turning point in my life because I recently made the decision to file bankruptcy after spending part one of my life on making money...acquiring stuff and looking good. Money, property, and prestige was my banner and looking good was my mantra at all costs...and cost it did. At forty-two every negative pattern that had been in play since I was fourteen had peaked. I had the clothes, done the travel, owned the business, and funded the relationships all so that you would think I was somebody. The last eight years were the inner work, which brings me to where I am now. I am somebody... and if you can't love me for who I am without the stuff then you're not supposed to be in my life. The decision to file bankruptcy was the final forgiveness I needed to give myself.... I would forgive someone else... how about me? I deserved a second chance, too. Yes, I still love money but I've completely restructured my life. At forty-three, the most important thing to me is love and the relationships in my life. They are the only things that you get to take with you.... the love you gave and the love you received, not the Armani suit we bought. So for me, I'm spending my life seeking my connection with my God... reaching into my heart to love my nearest and dearest.... and to love myself through it all.

Brenda's Life Bank

Forty-three years old
376,680 life hours spent

Her Life "Accounting"

Was a professional dance teacher in New York City, five years
Danced professionally on stage
Worked in the fashion business in New York

Traveled to China, Tibet, Hong Kong, Thailand, Holland, Germany, France, Italy, England, Austria, Brazil, Argentina, and Greece

Went to Paris to dance tango and met new friends

Chased tango from Paris to Argentina to San Francisco to Los Angeles

Created a dance event to have salsa and tango played

Produced fashion shows

Shopped the world for clients as an Image Consultant for five years

Have been clean and sober for more than eight years

Member of the Agape Church for ten years

Traveled to meet my spiritual teachers

Owned a large salon for five years

Have been a hairdresser for twenty years

Rowed on a crew

Was a body builder for four years

Learned to water ski

Snow skis with abandon

Lost and kept off twenty-two pounds

Created my own art studio

Been a painter for eight years

Have had four solo art shows

Sold almost all my work

Have been on my spiritual path for thirteen years

Have "count-on-able" relationships with my friends

Learned to meditate

Have been a godparent to my niece, Rachel

Became the sister I wanted to be to my brother and sister

Sang in my seventh- and eighth-grade school play

Learned to speak German and French

Genuinely loved the men in my life and grew with them

Envisioned winning the green card lottery for a friend and manifested it

Brenda is a wonderful example of someone who, through her commitment to her spiritual path and practice, discovered her true net worth. I know the journey was not easy for her, yet I have watched her fall down and pick herself up repeatedly. She never gives up. She is an Innocent who came to claim her power in the kingdom within, a necessary lesson for any who seek to become money Magicians.

Chapter 5

BUILDING A HEALTHY
RELATIONSHIP WITH MONEY

*Man is a knot, a web, a mesh into which relationships
are tied. Only those relationships matter.*

— St. Exupery, *Flight to Arras*, 1942

At the beginning of any new relationship, most mature, healthy adults reflect on their past relationships and the lessons they have learned. We seek understanding and desire to apply these lessons to our new relationships. Most of us do not wish to make the same mistakes over and over again. We want to get it right. However, the success of any future relationship greatly depends on our doing our own work, resolving our own issues, and clearing the way for the new relationship to evolve.

This is also true of your relationship with money. To have the relationship with money that you desire, you must first go through this clearing process. Just as not doing this process would probably result in the repeating

of old patterns and behavior in a new relationship, not
clearing the energy of past financial patterns and old
money energy will continue to sabotage your relationship with money. But first let's work to define your relationship with money.

DEFINING YOUR RELATIONSHIP TO MONEY

In working with my clients and their money issues, I
always begin by asking them to describe their relationship to money. Their responses often reveal clues about
their money types, which helps me to better understand
their money issues. Initially most people do not know
how to respond. It is rare that someone spontaneously
responds by saying, "Oh, I have a great relationship with
money. I understand it, I love having it in my life, and
it's not really a concern. I always have enough." Most
people do not think of money as something they have a
relationship to. I have a client who always used to say,
"I hate dealing with money; why would I want to have
a relationship with it?" To which I would reply, "You
don't always like your mother either, but you have a
relationship with her. It's just not always what you'd like
it to be. But she's in your life, and you never give up on
her. It's the same with money. Your job is to learn how
to make your relationship with money work for you, not
against you."

In truth, by definition, we have a relationship to anything that we are connected to or dependent on. Based
on those parameters, money qualifies as something we
have a relationship with. But besides spending an enor-
mous amount of our time thinking about it, worrying
about it, and working for it, we give money very little of

our attention. We base much of our self-worth on money, and since we undervalue the self, it makes sense that we have not paid enough attention to our relationship with money.

Every relationship that holds any significant value in our lives is a living energy system that needs attention, understanding, and nurturing. It is precisely our inattention to and lack of understanding of money that has caused us to have so much difficulty with and conflict about it. This is how our self-worth got to be diminished by our net worth to begin with. That which we do not give proper care and attention to generally does not respond well in return. If we don't water our plants, they whither and die. If we don't clean and maintain our living space, it becomes chaotic and unhealthy. If we don't care for and nurture our relationships with our friends and family, we risk hurting and losing those we love. If we neglect our work or career, we jeopardize our position and can end up unemployed. We must give focused energy and intention to all dimensions of our lives if we expect them to work.

I think it would be safe to say that because of our denial of what money means to us, most of us have unconsciously allowed our relationship with it to be shelved and to collect dust. I have often seen people retreat into fear or anger at the mere suggestion that perhaps they had problems with money they needed to look at. Everyone feels vulnerable when it comes to money. That we are fearful about it is not too surprising when we consider that we have never been properly educated about money or financial matters. We have no training in the one thing that our culture collectively values the most!

No wonder we respond in anger. We have been given the "power" and told we need to go out and "make it" without the proper tools. Statistically, money is among the leading causes of divorce and suicide. What does that say about us? Money affects every aspect of our lives, and yet we know very little about it. It is time to consciously choose to change this dynamic. A shift in our consciousness will not only help us to build stronger relationships with one another, but it will also be a step toward creating a new legacy for our children, one built on knowledge and power instead of fear and dependence. But first we must each define and redefine our relationship with money and its meaning in our lives. Let us turn to an examination of the true nature of money as part of this process.

THE NATURE OF MONEY

Money contains a powerful energy force. The road to abundance and prosperity requires that you first clear the path. To do so you must create an energy field in your own life that reflects and attracts the energy of money. Not unlike the attraction that exists between people, the energy of money is attracted to that which is most like itself. Let's begin by going through the process of clearly describing the qualities of money. The more clarity you have about all the traits of money, the easier it will be for you to consciously take on those same characteristics in your belief system. From here you can begin to create the space for money to enter your life. Money will become more accessible as you clear the channel and develop an entry way, one that was always there but was blocked by unconscious and unresolved issues. The path to unblocking requires that you understand and embrace the nature of money. Below I have listed some words that reflect the essence of money.

Money is:

- Alive
- Fluid
- Energetic
- Creative
- Powerful
- Transformational
- Attached to nothing

Money has always found its way into our hands first by means of creative intention, which is the process of moving creative thoughts, ideas, and imagination into form and action. We, as human beings, have repeatedly been offered the gift of money and all too often have not heeded the lessons of what came before us, resulting in the negative use of a creative, positive energy. Throughout history we have blamed money as the culprit for the ills of the time: war, famine, and economic collapse. Money however, was never the true cause. Lack of consciousness, greed, and hatred are not compatible energies with money. Money does not make people greedy. People make themselves greedy. Money does not create wars — people do.

MONEY AS CREATIVE FLOW

Money contains a creative energy that is attracted to that which is most like itself. Do not forget these words. For as long as you reflect the essence of these words in your life, you will always attract money. Fortunes are made and lost daily because people do not understand this basic principle and thus defeat themselves. If money is so creative, fluid, energetic, and so forth and is attracted to like qualities, why does so much of it often end up in the wrong hands? Well, money as an energy is not judgmental: It is detached. We think of creativity as only taking a positive form, but it can also manifest itself in negative forms. Money does not distinguish between the two. It simply follows the creative flow. Ultimately, though, most negative forms of creative energy are destructive. As we saw in chapter 2, throughout history, whenever money has been used to dominate and destroy or to limit the freedom of others, the flow of money has ceased and society has collapsed. The same dynamic continues today, in both people and governments.

The creative energy of money cannot sustain itself when the energy field becomes dark and money is no longer reflected in the forms around it. It is interesting to note that money itself, from an economic perspective, has the same problem. It requires constant attention and a fine balancing act of its ebb and flow. The major purpose of the Federal Reserve is to control the flow of money to the best of its ability. Too much flow of money creates inflation, when money is actually not worth as much. Too little flow creates a depression because there is not enough. The right flow, then, is when we possess neither too much or too little. We could all benefit from this understanding in our lives. Perhaps then not only our personal finances but also the world's economies would become stronger, healthier, and more attuned to positive creative energy.

CLEANING YOUR FINANCIAL HOUSE

When building your new relationship with money, it's important to start with a clean slate. To accomplish this, you will need to clean up your financial house and tie up any loose ends. Although this can be a painful process, depending on the degree of financial chaos in your life, it is essential in unblocking the flow of energy in your life. This process is also important because it helps you to free your mind and heart of any guilt, judgment, or negative feelings associated with both your past and current financial experiences. If you do not find a way to cleanse your mind of negative associations, they will continue to block the flow of creative energy, and this will be reflected in your future financial life as well. As architects of our own lives, and as collaborators with God, we need to build a solid foundation that is not compromised by the burdens of the past.

John's Story

The first time I met with my client John, he said, "I just want you to know up front that I don't trust anyone when it comes to money." I thanked him for letting me know that he distrusted me and suggested that it might be helpful for him to explain this lack of trust. He proceeded to tell me about how his former wife had ruined him financially and that his children only called him when they wanted money. He was in business with his father, and he too had cheated John out of money. John felt that everyone in his life had betrayed him over money, and he had become so mistrustful that protecting himself financially was his only goal in life.

As we talked for more than two hours, John slowly
began to express the grief and pain that was at the root
of his mistrust. At one point he began to cry, saying, "I
have given everything to everybody. I have taken care
of everyone... who's ever taken care of me?" Needless to
say, John operated from the Martyr money type. What he
did not understand was that he had used money as a
form of control, which he disguised as taking care of
those he loved. Unfortunately, his behavior had back-
fired. The expectation he had about those he had "sac-
rificed and helped" resulted in various forms of
emotional retaliation and financial consequences. John
had failed to understand how he had used money as a
measure of his love. Rather than actually being loving
and giving of himself, he had either rewarded or withheld money as a substitute for the love that he did not
know how to give. It was no surprise that money was all
he had left. Sadly, his relationship with money (as a form
of control) not only masked his real love for others but
also prevented him from receiving the love he needed.
Deep down, John did not believe he was lovable. He
ended up manifesting a self-fulfilling prophecy of financial betrayal as proof that no one really loved him, that
it was his money they sought and loved. However,
regardless of people's attempts to exchange money for
love, money can never replace the real expression of
love that comes from the heart.

Over time John learned to relate to his children by
truly being there for them emotionally and not simply
financially. His relationship with his children was actually a mirror of the relationship he had had with his own
father. His father had also demonstrated his love and

approval with money, an example of how an archetypal pattern is passed along from one generation to the next. It is not easy work to change a lifetime behavior pattern, let alone one that has been in the family for a few generations. John had to be willing to look at his own part in creating the dynamic in his relationships rather than live in the shadow of the past. Eventually, he was able to rebuild his trust by redefining his relationship with money and with the people he cared for in his life, including his father. As he released his feelings of anger and betrayal, he was able to access his grief and experience his real loss, which was not the loss of money, but the loss of love. Money Therapy helped John to discover that he was not seeking to protect his money. He was seeking to protect his heart.

TAKING INVENTORY OF YOUR FINANCIAL LIFE

It is almost impossible to change your relationship with money without cleaning up the emotional business of your past. One way to do this is to take an inventory of your financial life. Begin by writing down a list of any unfinished financial issues that you want to resolve. This process may include confronting people you love or care about. Remember to include items that you don't completely feel responsible for (for example, a bill that continues to haunt you that you feel is inaccurate or a tax assessment you disagree with). When you are finished, number these unresolved issues in order of their importance and/or the pressure they put on you. Take the top three items from that list and make a "take action" list. Put the first list away for now. For each of the three items on this list, make a decision to take some positive action

to resolve it within the next week. Focus on resolution
and contact each person, business, and so on and say,
"I'm calling to let you know that my intention is to
resolve this issue. This is my situation. How can we
work this out?" Continue this process until you find a
way to work through your entire list. Try to resist taking
on more tasks than you can handle, because doing so
may drain you physically and emotionally. The goal of
this exercise is to help you feel good about handling
unfinished business, not to make you feel bad.

There's a chance that not every situation will work
out exactly as you intended. But having everything work
out perfectly is not the sole purpose of this exercise. It
is more important that you consciously make your intentions known and that you act on those intentions. The
mere act of putting your intention and desire to work to
shift this energy will create an opening for new energy
to be channeled back into you. Your faith and connection to Spirit will help facilitate the rest.

Please note: If you are having great difficulty with
this process, it may be a sign that you need outside assistance. Do not hesitate to contact a counselor or seek
legal or financial assistance if it will help you get the job
done. By whatever means it takes, the end result will be
the same: You will feel lighter, have more energy, and
be ready to lay a new foundation for your future relationship with money.

One client of mine, a classic Innocent type who took
the ostrich approach to money matters, was so completely overwhelmed by her financial problems she was
on the verge of a nervous breakdown by the time she
came to me. Consumed by bills and debt, she had

stopped opening her mail because she simply could not cope with her circumstances. This, of course, only served to make matters worse, because whether she opened them or not, they still existed and grew larger over time. She was paralyzed with fear and guilt.

One piece at a time, we began to sift through her unopened mail only to discover that the amount she really needed to pay every month to keep her obligations was fairly manageable. Her problem was that she felt so guilty about her spending habits and so overwhelmed by the large quantity of bills that she became overwhelmed and unable to respond rationally. She ended up hiring a credit counselor, who negotiated payments with her creditors, and an accountant to file her back taxes. She made one payment every month for two years, and it was over. In the meantime, we continued to do Money Therapy.

In time she began to unravel her personal history and saw how her spending habits were rooted in her unhappiness in her relationship. She had been involved with a man for many years who she loved deeply but who had always been emotionally unavailable and unwilling to commit. Her spending habits grew out of her need to fill up the places where she was unfulfilled in her relationship. Buying things for herself gave her the feeling of being loved and nurtured. For a time, she felt valued. However, as she received less and less from her relationship, she bought more and more for herself, a dynamic that led to completely shattering her self-esteem and creating a financial crisis. In this circumstance, money became a substitute for the love she was missing and craving. In that way, it also became an addiction.

She became a member of Debtor's Anonymous, and the benefits of that program helped her immensely.

She eventually left her boyfriend and resurrected her life in the form of a new career in advertising. She now owns a highly successful advertising company and makes more than $300,000 a year. She cleaned up her financial house, cleared her life of negative emotional energy, and applied her lessons to building the world she wanted to inhabit. There had been no room for this life before. First she had to create the space for it. Once she did this, the creative flow of money simply followed her there.

EXERCISE

Looking for Your Perfect Money Relationship

◆◆◆◆◆◆◆◆◆◆◆◆◆◆◆◆◆◆◆◆◆◆◆◆◆◆◆◆◆◆

Using relationships as the metaphor, begin to think about what kind of money relationship you are seeking. If you were to place a personal ad in the newspaper seeking a partner, you would want to have a pretty clear idea of what you're looking for beforehand. Otherwise, you're not likely to receive what you are looking for. The clearer you are about what you want, the more likely you are to manifest whatever relationship you desire, whether it be with a person, a job, or money. So be clear about what kind of relationship you desire to have with money. Write a personal ad that addresses your intention. Here's an example: "Spiritual being seeking a relationship with money that is trustworthy, fulfilling, cocreative, prosperous, and knows no limits. I am ready to receive this relationship into my life and to embrace this prosperity with care and attention so that together we may realize our greatest good."

When you have written your ad, tape it to your bathroom mirror. Read this written intention aloud every morning as you prepare for your day. As you finish reading it, repeat the following words: "I am willing to receive this perfect relationship into my life and consider it done, and so it will be."

Chapter 6

LOVE AND POWER,
FEAR AND CONTROL

For one human being to love another: that is perhaps the most difficult of all our tasks, the ultimate, the last test and proof, the work for which all other work is but preparation.

— Rainer Marie Rilke, *Letters to a Young Poet*, 1904

As human beings, we alone have the deep need to control the world around us. Fairly early in life, we learn to fear and mistrust what we cannot predict or control. We are uncomfortable with and wary in the presence of contradiction, which is why, I believe, we have such difficulty with money. Money is filled with contradiction. It has a duality that is not unlike our own nature as human beings. It is both spiritual and material, creative and destructive, loving and cruel. It has the capacity to help us fulfill our greatest dreams or be defeated by our worst nightmare.

EMBRACING MONEY'S DUALITY

If we are to heal our relationship with money, we must learn to embrace its shadows as well as its light. For money is but another mirror that reflects the energy of its beholder. It is essential that we acknowledge this truth so that we can consciously choose which side of its reality we want to live in and create. We must be willing to embrace this duality to understand it and to become familiar with its many dimensions and inherent contradictions. Everything in life is a metaphorical puzzle of some sort. What we see and believe is real on the surface is often quite another thing. As I look out on the horizon, I see acres of flat land stretched out before me. For a moment I can truly understand why it was once believed that the world was flat. But the world is not flat, and neither is money. Money, like the world, is multidimensional. Until we begin to alter our perspective, we will continue to live in a one-dimensional self-sabotaging world in which money is represented as either one thing or another, good or evil, black or white. This is not, however, the truth, nor does it serve us to believe it.

Money permeates every part of our existence and affects not only our relationship with our self but also our relationship to others. To a great extent, we unconsciously make our money decisions from a position of love or power, fear or control. Far too often, the decisions we make about money are based on fear because when it comes to money, most of us feel out of control. However, fear-based money decisions are reactions, not choices. These fear-based reactions come from our need to control and are therefore lacking in any real power. When we make conscious choices about money based on loving our self and others, we stand in the power and presence of Spirit and can trust that all our needs will be met.

CHANGING HOW WE THINK ABOUT MONEY

The world is filled with images of people who have climbed the ladder of success at the expense of others and have been willing to sell their souls for financial gain, power, and control. We are given the message that only the financially strong survive. These images, combined with our collective history, have served only to deepen the level of mistrust of and disdain for money. Years of accumulated experience, both personal and societal, have unconsciously prevented us from manifesting our rightful abundance. Our negative and fearful associations with money conspire against us and sabotage our efforts at creating the life and financial security we greatly desire. For this state to shift, we must re-create a belief system filled with positive images along with a language that supports and reinforces the reality we wish to manifest. For not only do we house negative associations in our mind, we also give them life through the language we often use, further blocking the flow of money from our lives.

Just as our thoughts about money are infinitely powerful, our words are even more so. A thought followed by words has creative energy and movement behind it. As it moves from an intention to an action, it grows infinitely more powerful. If we are to learn to tap into the power we possess to create our reality, we must become conscious of the content of our mind, words, intentions, and actions.

There are many simple things we can do to learn how to do this. For example, when you are experiencing a shortage of money flow, don't automatically say, "I'm broke." Instead, try to state your circumstances in a more positive manner, such as "I'm having a money recess. That just means I need to play more and spend less." When your children ask for something, don't give them the old "money doesn't grow on trees" cliché. Tell them the truth. Tell them that money is an important resource and we need to be careful how we use it. If they cry because you won't buy something, console them and tell them you love them but that we don't show love by buying things. Through love, we can teach our children to be fulfilled from within.

CHANGING HOW WE THINK ABOUT OURSELVES

People often display behavior that is confusing and contradictory to their nature with regard to money. This behavior represents unconscious and unresolved issues that become manifested in our money types. Money can and does bring out the best and worst in us. It is this duality that we must seek to become more conscious of. When we can own our own duality and contradictions, we can begin to consciously choose where and how we want to live. Both the light and the dark exist within us. To deny this is to deny a part of ourselves. We can choose to experience what we are conscious of; we can even create our own reality. However, what we deny has a life of its own, chipping away at us internally like a prisoner trying to escape from his own private hell. We must learn to merge the inner, spiritual world with the outer, material world or risk becoming prisoners of our own making.

Allen's Story

The key to changing our financial reality lies in our ability to recognize the unconscious patterns and beliefs that we act out in our everyday lives, primarily through our money types. It is interesting to witness how an otherwise loving and kind person can take on a quite different persona when it comes to money. A poignant example of this was displayed by a client of mine named Allen, who came to see me at the insistence of his wife, who was upset and frustrated by what she referred to as his "financial stubbornness." Allen was an extremely capable and intelligent man. He had a wife and a son whom he loved very much, and he owned a successful business. Both of his parents had died many years before I met him, and he had inherited a substantial amount of money. This money could have created a lot of security and comfort for Allen and his family, but instead it became the source of much family stress, in particular with his relationship with his son, Josh. Although Allen had the financial means, he was adamant about not paying for Josh's college education. It was "his" money, and he did not feel that he should have to pay for his son's education beyond high school.

Allen also had a tremendous resistance to investing. Since receiving his inheritance, he had also developed some rather excessive spending habits. By the time I met him, he had spent a great deal of his inheritance and only had $150,000 in liquid assets left, which had been sitting in a money market account and earning a mere 4 percent in interest. The bulk of his inheritance went to purchasing two pieces of real estate, which included the home they lived in and his childhood family vacation home on the coast of Maine. Allen had paid in cash for both properties. The family had not visited the home in Maine more than a couple of times, and they had not rented it out. The combined value of the properties was over $600,000. The family had almost no other investments except a small IRA account that Allen had started years ago. On the surface, one might not think that this is such a bad scenario, but there is more here than meets the eye.

When I asked Allen how he felt about investing, he proceeded to tell me that his father was a "gambler" who always played the stock market. Unfortunately, his father "lost the game," and part of the money he had lost had been promised to Allen for his college education. Shortly thereafter, his father had died, leaving Allen feeling even more cheated. After his father's death, Allen's mother, who had never managed money before, hired a stockbroker to assist her, and according to Allen, the stockbroker "swindled" his mother out of much of her money. I listened to this story empathitically, since these events had clearly affected Allen, although he showed no visible signs of emotion. When he had finished talking, I told him that considering his history, his resistance to investing was understandable. He response was, "I might not be doing as well as I could, but it's my money, and I'm doing it my way." His words helped me to understand why his wife had referred to him as "financially stubborn." At this point, I began to suspect that Allen was a money Tyrant.

I proceeded to redirect the conversation to Allen's current financial concerns and priorities. He told me that he wanted to begin to retire when he was fifty (he was forty-four at the time) and that other than putting his son through private school, he didn't really have any other priorities. I asked him about planning for his son's college education, and he said flatly that he would not pay for it. I did not respond to the obvious contradiction that Allen was willing to spend a great deal of money on private high school but stopped short of spending a dime on college. He obviously felt committed to his son's education or he would not have paid for private school. This lack of follow-through was odd, especially since he could easily afford it. I continued to probe.

Over the course of our lengthy meeting, it became clear to me that Allen still harbored some anger and resentment toward his father for gambling away his college education. At the end of our meeting I said, "I'm sorry about your experience with your father, but I must say for someone who didn't go to college, you're a very capable and intelligent man. You should feel good about yourself. You've done very well."

Looking rather stunned, Allen said, "Well, thanks, but I never said I didn't go to college. I graduated from Princeton." At that moment Allen had revealed his money type and the underlying cause of the problems he experienced with money. Allen was operating from a combination Victim/Tyrant type. Although he displayed all the main characteristics of the Victim type, the Tyrant had begun to manifest itself in direct proportion to Allen's unwillingness to deal with his true feelings. Allen was still playing out the emotional energy and anger he had toward his father. That his father really was a gambler is also suspect. It appeared that there was still plenty of money left after he died. However, Allen had to blame the loss of his father on something, and at some point Allen made an unconscious agreement with himself that he would never be a "gambler" like his father or never be "taken" like his mother. In spite of his reality, Allen still clung to the belief that he had somehow been deprived, and he blamed this deprivation on "money and investing." In this way he was also a Victim. Since his father had "gambled" and his mother had been "swindled," money was obviously the culprit.

Of course, Allen had not actually been deprived of anything. He went to one of the most prestigious schools in the country, and he had a trust fund. He was happily married and had a wonderful son. But deep inside he was a hurt little boy who felt let down by his father, and rather than face his pain, he projected his pain onto his relationship with money. The Victim at play in his financial life caused him to remain stuck in the past, where he stubbornly refused to let go of false beliefs — so much so that he had isolated his son, who felt rejected by his father's refusal to assist him with his education. Josh had performed very well academically, and his father had always stressed the importance of getting a good education. Without his father's help, he could not afford to attend any of the schools he had been accepted to and would most likely have to go to the nearby community college. This situation was hard to believe, since Allen so clearly loved his son. In addition, Allen refused to acknowledge his wife's concern about his spending and her fear that their money was not properly diversified. In denial of his true feelings, an otherwise thoughtful and loving man had turned into a Tyrant.

I worked with Allen for a few months. Eventually, he became conscious of how he had allowed his past experiences to contribute to his dysfunctional belief system about money. Somewhere deep inside Allen, the hurt and betrayal he felt toward his father had become transferred to money, even though the losses he had suffered were purely emotional and not financial. His parents had both died too soon. But rather than feel his grief, he had let himself become a Victim. The money represented all that remained of his parents, and although on the surface he appeared selfish, he really wasn't. He was afraid. The truth was that he didn't trust himself with money, and he didn't want to risk letting down his family, so he bought property and made no other financial plans and no financial promises because of his secret fear that he would fail. Allen's story is a great example of someone who is hiding their inner reality while unconsciously seeking comfort in the material world. It also shows how unresolved financial issues often become manifested in behavior that is contradictory to our true natures.

The greatest healing we can ever experience occurs when we can forgive. As Allen began to understand and forgive his parents, he opened his heart and chose to love his parents and be grateful for the opportunities they had given him. When he could see the truth about his parents, he could integrate it into his life. Allen's real healing came when he decided to set aside sufficient funds for his son's college education, which showed that he had truly forgiven his father and let go of the past. Over time, I taught him how to be a prudent investor. His overspending ceased as he realized that he could do well with money and was not destined to repeat the past. Allen refinanced their vacation home in Maine and rented it out. The rent covered the mortgage, and he and his wife invested $250,000 in equity. In the last ten years the money he invested grew to almost a million dollars. In that same period, the value of the real estate only increased about $100,000. Allen's change of heart undoubtedly made him more prosperous. Most important, it also saved Allen's relationship with his son. If Allen had not been willing to work on his money issues, chances are the Tyrant that had become activated would have become the dominating type in his life. Instead, he was able to become a money Magician. Fortunately, Allen chose love over fear and in doing so surrendered his need to control. Love is always infinitely more powerful than fear. Healing his relationship with money allowed Allen to pass on a new money legacy to his son, one of a money Magician, based on love and compassion, not fear and control.

COUPLES AND MONEY

Our unresolved money issues perhaps become most magnified in our relationships with others. Money and sex are the two most powerful energies that exist between human beings and are at the root of most relationship problems. In fact, it is far easier for most people to discuss sex than it is to discuss money, which is by far more taboo and kept considerably more hidden. In my observation, in both cases, the problem is one of supply and demand, in that whenever the supply is low, the demand usually gets stronger. People caught in this dynamic are usually acting out of lack and limitation, and their fear leads them to want more control. When we learn to act from a position of love and power, we become more open and available to truly receiving the abundance of life.

I think it would be safe to say that most of us have unconsciously allowed our relationship with money to whither because of our denial of what money means to us. I have seen many clients retreat into fear or anger at the mere suggestion that perhaps they had some issues with money that they needed to look at. Although it is a generalization, I have noticed that women mostly respond with fear, and men with anger. No doubt this is a result of considerable social conditioning, since historically women were (and to some extent still are) financially dependent on men and felt powerless over their lives and financial destinies. As I mentioned in chapter 3, many women are money Innocents. They aren't supposed to know about money because that's the "man's job." Although as women we have certainly made significant headway in the workplace, many of us still feel inadequate and unprepared when it comes to money.

For many women who are stay-at-home wives and

mothers, the financial decision making has remained
largely in their husbands' hands. In a traditional relationship, the husband works to support the family and
also makes most of the major financial decisions. While
gender roles have begun to evolve, change has been
slow to come, partially, I believe, because women are
afraid of asserting themselves in their relationships about
money. They often feel vulnerable about their financial
security and uncomfortable questioning their spouses'
financial decisions. I have seen many otherwise strong
women become quite subservient to their husbands
when it comes to money. As women, we tend to be the
emotional caretakers of our relationships. Since money
brings up so many issues, we feel it is better left undis-
turbed. Although it is far easier not to be the one in
charge of financial matters, remaining ignorant is not to
the benefit of most relationships.

I have worked with many couples to help them create healthier, more balanced agreements about money. I
enjoy this part of my work, because I can clearly see
how relieved couples become when they make an effort
to balance the power in the relationship. This kind of
balance can only be achieved when both people agree
to approach problems from a position of love and kind-
ness, especially when it comes to their partner's fears
and apprehensions. In the course of this work, I have
observed three common relationship money patterns,
which I will describe below.

The traditional pattern. The traditional pattern is
still by far the most common. This pattern most com-
monly duplicates our parents' money dynamic (or at
least our picture of it). In the traditional pattern, the

husband takes the lead in the financial decision making. Although the couple may talk about money and finances, especially any big decisions (like buying a house or a car), the final decision is almost always determined by the man. This pattern is not only common in relationships in which the husband works and the wife stays at home, but it is also prevalent in many two-income households. I have asked many women how they feel about this type of arrangement, and for the most part, although they would like to have equal say, they don't feel knowledgeable enough about money to insist upon having it.

The contemporary pattern. The contemporary pattern is the second most common I've observed among the couples I've worked with. In this type of relationship, the couple makes their financial decisions by joint agreement. This arrangement is more common amongst higher-income professionals, when both the husband and wife have a higher level of financial awareness and sophistication. This type of pattern lends itself to a higher level of communication and feeling of security and trust. That is not to say that people in this type of relationship do not also experience difficulties with money. However, since an agreement of inclusion already exists, no one partner has exclusive control over money decisions.

The financially autonomous pattern. The financially autonomous pattern is the least common, but it may be the fastest growing. I have observed this pattern most often in relationships between people who have been previously married or in other long-term relationships, are older, and have considerable financial assets that existed before their current relationship. In these relationships, the couple makes their financial decisions separately, and their finances and incomes are not commingled. No doubt the high level of divorce and the intricacies of the legal system have made many people cautious about forming financial attachments. I have seen this dynamic work both positively and negatively in relationships. Couples who are very clear about their individual financial security handle this type of arrangement quite well. However, not many people, regardless of how much money they have, feel financially secure. And often the person with less money often thinks that the partner with the most should contribute more to the household. Therefore, issues of trust and intimacy can also be common in financially autonomous relationships.

The following is an example of a couple I worked with in a traditional money relationship.

Stan and Diane's Story

I had worked with Stan and Diane as their financial advisor for many years before I began doing Money Therapy with them. They were great clients to work with, because they had such a loving relationship and I admired how well they communicated. Then one day they came to see me, and it was obvious that they were in a lot of conflict about money.

Stan was a prominent doctor, and Diane stayed at home taking care of their three children and managing the household affairs. Stan operated as a Warrior type and was very watchful of their financial well-being. Diane was a classic Innocent money type who was financially dependent on her husband. She had let go of her teaching career early in their marriage to care for their children. Although Diane was a vibrant and confident woman, when it came to money she looked up to her husband like a wide-eyed child. As we began to discuss their situation, Diane began to cry and became almost inconsolable. Stan explained that while trying to refinance their house he discovered that Diane had not been honest with him: She had been spending money and hiding the bills. That was hard enough to deal with, but as it turns out, Diane had also been late paying the hidden bills and had bounced quite a few checks, which had affected their credit and was making it difficult for them to refinance their home.

Stan felt betrayed and angry. Diane felt guilty and humiliated. I explained to them that their problem was not at all uncommon. I asked Stan if we could spend some time hearing from Diane how this situation had come about, because she was obviously in pain and needed to talk. I said to Diane, "I know you feel bad about what happened, but its important that you talk about what caused this problem. You must really be afraid or you wouldn't have needed to hide. Do you know what you are afraid of?" Diane began to talk through her tears about how hard it was living in constant fear of not having enough money. She said, "Stan always works so hard to provide for us, but I feel like we're in over our heads and that we're barely making it. Stan's been giving me the same amount of money every month for years to manage the house and kids, but it just keeps getting more and more expensive. I thought I could juggle it and not tell him I needed more. I don't want to put any more of the burden on him. I think I should get a job to help out, but he doesn't want me to work. So I started using credit cards and hoped I could pay them off a little at a time. But then I got behind and I got scared, and now it's all blown up in my face. I know it was wrong, but I was only trying to make things easier."

At this point, I was confused. I asked Stan if they were having financial difficulties, and he said, "Well, my practice is down a little, but we're okay. We just have to cut back a bit. That's why I was refinancing the house." Clearly Diane's emotional conflict was not congruent with their external financial reality. They did not lack for money. Stan made a very good living, they owned a beautiful home, and they had a considerable amount of money invested. I asked Diane why she thought they were in financial trouble. In the course of our discussion, the source of their problem was revealed.

Stan had been so afraid that Diane would "mess up" their finances that he gave her a monthly allowance and handled all other money matters himself. Diane's personal history, mostly her childhood, with money was chaotic, and Stan knew that as a result she was fearful about money. Consequently, he seldom discussed money with her — he just handled it. Occasionally, he would comment that his practice was down or that the market was down, just in passing conversation. Diane took what he said to mean that they had financial problems. Since like a true Warrior Stan went out of his way to shield his wife from money matters, Diane never knew if they had money or not. Left to her own fear-based devices, she became truly convinced they were in financial jeopardy. She chose not to inform Stan that her "allowance" to cover the household expenses was not enough because she felt he was already working too hard. So she hid her spending and the bills, and the problem grew out of control. Stan was acting more like a parent than a partner. As it turns out, that was exactly how his father had handled money in his family.

By not including Diane in their financial life, Stan not only prevented his wife from growing up financially, but he actually added to her fear. I worked with Stan and Diane to establish a healthier system of managing their money based on an understanding of each other's needs and fears. Stan agreed to give Diane a check for their household account that was more than they actually needed. He also agreed to give her a check for her own account, since she was uncomfortable asking for what she needed.

I feel strongly that as adults, it is an unhealthy setup if either partner has to ask for money from the other. This type of arrangement is damaging to the individual's self-esteem and to the relationship. In this case, Stan was very open to seeing his part in creating their problems and really wanted to help his wife become as strong in money matters as she was in other areas of her life. Stan really loved Diane, but he secretly withheld money from her out of fear that she would mismanage it. The monthly check he gave her left no room for error, which terrified her. He also withheld information from her, which only gave her the opportunity to form false conclusions that sabotaged them both.

This couple agreed to hire an outside consultant to help them organize their financial records, bring them current, and then perform a quarterly "maintenance" of the system. Having this help brought their anxiety level down considerably. Essentially, they had instituted an outside checks-and-balances system so that they could keep any negative money energy out of their marriage. Over time, Stan began to act less like the "father" and more like a partner, and Diane grew more secure about money. Both Stan and Diane needed to bring their relationship with money into consciousness. Eventually, they were able to discard their old patterns and beliefs and replace them with a system that better served them both as individuals and as a couple.

Stan and Diane forgave each other for the roles they had played in creating their circumstances. It was heartwarming to witness Stan drop his anger and to approach his wife with compassion and love. He clearly understood why Diane had become so fearful and how his own need for control had contributed to her fear. They had each brought their own money issues into the marriage, which they continued to act out unconsciously until a crisis had occurred. In this case, the crisis was a blessing in disguise that ultimately led to deeper love and understanding between them.

It is a truly rewarding experience when Money Therapy works out this way. I have watched too many relationships where couples use money as a form of control. Unfortunately, the energy of control is constrictive and undermines the love and trust between people. If we can stand together and face these challenges in our lives with love and compassion, we will develop more powerful bonds and have increasing access to the flow of abundance.

EXERCISE

Money Therapy for Couples

◆◆◆◆◆◆◆◆◆◆◆◆◆◆◆◆◆◆◆◆◆◆◆◆◆◆◆◆◆◆◆◆◆◆

The following exercise will help you understand how the relationship your parents had with money is reflected in your own life and relationships. In many cases, this exercise has helped my clients discover the source of money issues that are rooted in childhood memories and experiences.

Questions to Ask Yourselves Separately

1. How did your parents handle money? Were they open about it or secretive?
2. Did you grow up feeling that money was abundant or scarce?
3. What money type best describes your mother? Your father?
4. Was money a frequent source of conflict between your parents?
5. Did you frequently sense that either of your parents were worried or fearful about money?
6. Do you remember being worried or feeling afraid about money yourself?
7. What words or phrases were used about money by your parents or by other significant relatives?

Once you have both separately answered these questions, share your responses. Take turns reading your responses out loud to each other. Each partner should pay close attention to the emotional responses the other displays. This process can be heart opening and revealing. You may be learning something completely new about your partner. He or she may become vulnerable in a way you've never seen. You may witness a lot of residual pain, a sign that your partner needs your love and compassion to help him or her heal. To the extent that you are willing to offer this love, your relationship will grow stronger and more powerful. Any money issues that have arisen in your relationship can be overcome when you stand in the light and power of love.

Questions to Ask As a Couple

Now that you asked yourselves the above questions as individuals and shared your answers with each other, sit down together and answer the following questions as a couple:

1. How do you handle money as a couple?
2. Are you in a traditional, contemporary, or autonomous relationship?
3. Are you satisfied with this pattern?
4. If not, what pattern would you prefer, and why?
5. Is money a frequent source of conflict in your relationship?

6. Do you feel your partner is often worried or fearful about money?
7. What words or phrases do you hear yourself or your partner use about money?
8. Are any of these on your lists from childhood?
9. Do you have any children? How do you think they would answer these questions about your relationship with money? Pretend you are each other's child. What would you like your child to feel and believe about money? Tell each other. If you have children, tell them.

We must learn to tell the truth about money, to each other, to our children, and to the world. We need to build a new foundation for money in our lives. We need to provide our children with a healthy level of money awareness as they grow. It is time to bring money out of the closet and into our lives, homes, and hearts in new and empowering ways. It is time to choose love over fear, and to surrender rather than to control. For in choosing the light, we leave little room for the darkness to appear and if it does, we need not be afraid for we possess the power to extinguish it.

Chapter 7

THE PATH TO FULFILLMENT

Rise up nimbly and go on your strange journey.

— Rumi, "The Real Work," thirteenth century

The patterns influencing our relationship with money begin when we are children, which is also when we receive our first glimpse of fulfillment reflected in the mirror of the material world. As children we often make unconscious agreements about money that affect the choices we make about our personal path as adults. By the time most children are in elementary school, they have already begun to identify money as an important source for getting their needs met. Adults perpetuate this belief by providing children with an endless supply of material proof of their love and affection. And with each passing birthday and holiday, the bar gets raised a little higher, until it becomes increasingly difficult to meet the expectations we have created in our children. Consequently, they grow up believing that fulfillment is an external, material reality that can be bought with money.

We have so confused money with fulfillment that the very meaning of the word has been lost. Fulfillment can only be truly experienced internally. It is not something you can acquire or buy. It is not a place you can fill full enough with stuff to take you there. Fulfillment is about completion and self-realization. It is more a process than a destination. It is not something anyone can give you; it is something you become.

LOSING OUR WAY

One of the ways we can experience true fulfillment comes from the deep knowing in your soul that you are on your path and understand your life's purpose. Unfortunately, we are often so disconnected from our own souls that we have difficulty finding our path and often stop searching for it. We may even stop believing that we have a soul at all. Too few of us were nurtured to become what would fulfill us personally or spiritually. This is an unfortunate reality, because we all need guidance and encouragement in developing our awareness and acceptance of who we are and the gifts we possess. To know your uniqueness is powerful indeed. To not know it leaves a hollow space that too many of us simply attempt to fill in other ways.

When we are children, our memory of the Spirit is still fresh. Our connection to God and our souls is so close to the surface that we can experience our inner light easily and joyfully. Although small in size, children possess large gifts and unlimited potential. As adults we must encourage children to explore these gifts while the information is most accessible and before they become self-conscious of their spirituality. Children are nearer to their spiritual selves simply because they have occupied their human bodies for less time than adults have, which is undoubtedly why they are notorious for revealing the truth. Children come from truth, and it remains the only reality they know until we teach them otherwise. To watch a small child at play is to witness a soul expressing itself effortlessly. Until one day children lose their innocence and imperceptibly the person steps in and overshadows the soul. However, the soul is eternal and will deliver us back to our true selves, our true lives, and our true paths. The soul represents the fulfillment that is revealed when we are living in truth and in accordance with our purpose.

As children we did not experience ourselves as separate from others; we felt connected to everything around us. For this brief time, we all knew true freedom. This freedom did not require money. As we grew up, we became self-conscious as we were increasingly defined by the people around us, namely, our parents, family, and friends. We were told who we were or were not in relationship to others and our experience of them. We became known as "good," "bad," "sweet," "smart," or whatever adjectives the people we looked up to, literally, used to describe us. We have become unconscious of the powerful effect that words and language have on our psyches and self-esteem. This lack of consciousness is particularly harmful to children, who display the psychic wounds inflicted by language so early in life. It is no small wonder that our souls retreat so easily into the background of our lives. As our center of truth, the soul is vulnerable to the untruths we are told and submerges into a deeper, more protective space. This experience marks the beginning of our disconnectedness and explains why so many of us have difficulty finding our way.

By the time we reach adulthood, many of us have lost access to the truth that lies inside the retreated soul and have become simply what we were expected to be. We take jobs, create careers, marry, have children, and so on largely based on unconscious agreements with people in our daily lives and those who have influenced us. As it turns out, living this way works for some people. But many others yearn for something more.

FINDING OUR PATH

Somewhere along the way, the sleeping soul grows restless and longs to finally express the truth of who we really are. It becomes the still, small voice within that says, "Wait a minute, this isn't the life I wanted. This isn't who I really am! How did I get here? How do I get out?" And suddenly we begin to question our life's choices and look around at the world we've created and to feel trapped. At a certain point, we often realize that we bought a ticket to a life that we no longer wish to live but that there is no refund.

As a Warrior type I have fought being defined by anyone and have always felt compelled to help others find their paths. From an early age I knew that I had a purpose and destiny. I did not, however, have a clue what it was. I was born with an intuitive gift of seeing the truth in others. In my work, this gift has frequently allowed me to "see" if someone is on his or her true path. Sometimes I can see the obstacle blocking the person from their path. I rarely reveal this information directly to people but work instead to facilitate their own discovery of it by opening the door.

We are blessed when we are truly seen and appreciated for who we are. We all need people to hold the space for our greater truth to be known until we can see it for ourselves. Finding our way back to our path and purpose can be a lifelong journey. Some people are lucky and discover it early in life. However, most of us struggle with this journey and often fall down or get lost along the way. And that's okay. There is no such thing as a mistake when you are truly working toward finding your path. What matters is that you keep making the effort. Our task is to simply keep moving toward the light until we can see. In the thirteenth century, the great Sufi poet and philosopher Rumi wrote:

> There is one thing in this world that you must never forget to do. If you forget everything else and not this, there's nothing to worry about; but if you remember everything else and forget this, then you will have done nothing in your life. It is as if a king has sent you to some country do a task, and you perform a hundred other services, but not the one he sent you to do. So human beings come to this world to do particular work. The work is the purpose, and each is specific to the person.[1]

---

[1] Jalal Al-Din Rumi, *The Illuminated Rumi*. Translated and with commentary by Coleman Barks. (New York: Broadway Books, 1997), p. 24.

Although the truth is eternal, it not easy to find if we are busy looking for something else. If you're trying to find your path, it will be easier to discover if you stop expecting it to be clothed in money. I often ask the people I work with what took them off their path. They usually answer with conviction that "there's no money in it" or that they "cannot afford to make the change." I can only tell you what I know to be true: You cannot afford *not* to make the change. The price for not changing is far higher than you'll ever know. We can only turn away the gift of our divinity so many times before it is no longer offered.

People come to me wanting to make changes in their lives. They feel they are off course and want to seek a new direction but are uncertain about how to go about it. They frequently feel trapped by their choices. More often than not they feel their only ticket to freedom is money. If only they had enough money, they could make that change. Most people believe that money will cure their problems, will buy them out of the life they're living and into the life they desire. Money is the magic wand, the solution to all our problems. Many of us believe it is the answer to the prayers we often forget to pray.

During the course of our lives, as we have become increasingly disconnected from Spirit, we have lost access to our power. We have become blind to the light within us. The more we have placed our trust and faith in the outside world, the darker and more unfamiliar our inner world has grown. Without the unrelenting voice of the soul, which constantly seeks our attention and never stops trying to redirect us back to our path, we would never find our way. We all possess an inner compass: We just have forgotten how to use it. The soul doesn't say, "Follow me, I'll show you the way to the money." It just says, "Follow me, I'll show you the way." Forget about money! It will show up when it is time. Our task is to simply heed the signs and follow the directions provided by the Spirit within.

PROSPERITY AND ABUNDANCE

When we are on the right path, all our needs are met in abundance. Before I go any further, I should say that the words *abundance* and *prosperity* are not the same and need to be clarified. Abundance is our most natural state. To have abundance means having plenty or more than enough. Yet the concept of "enough" is what creates a dilemma for most of us. Abundance is very subjective, since what one person considers plenty is a mere pittance to another. Prosperity, on the other hand, is a little easier to define. To be prosperous means to be "successful or fortunate." We have come to believe that being truly prosperous requires "having a fortune." As a result many people live in a state of abundance without knowing it, because they were seeking the "fortune" of prosperity. In my experience, prosperity does not come easily to those who wait for it or seek it out specifically. Prosperity is what happens to people while they're busy doing other things. If our actions are connected to our path, then we are truly fortunate, for we will know the joy of prosperity that comes from fulfillment. The following questions will help you examine and distinguish between prosperity and abundance as they relate to fulfillment in your life.

Do you feel abundance in your life?
If not, what do you feel is missing?
Do you feel you are prosperous?
What does prosperity look like to you?
What makes you feel fulfilled?
What remains unfulfilled within you?
What are you willing to do to change that today?

RECHOOSING YOUR PATH TO FULFILLMENT

Fear of moving from the known — even if we don't like it — into the unknown prevents most of us from realizing the magic and wonder of being on our true path. Every day I encounter people who allow fear to keep them from moving forward into the uncertainty of the path that lies before them. It helps to keep in mind that we are all already on a path. Not one of us is an accident. Even if we were not all "planned" by our parents, that does not make any one of us anything less than a miracle. We were not just created because God needed extra people to take up space. God doesn't make mistakes. Everyone and everything has a purpose.

We each have a gift to give — a unique part of us that no one else can give. When we have discovered, or, more accurately, uncovered this part of ourselves, we truly begin to shine. I believe that we often get lost while searching for who we really are and our true path because of the misguided belief that they must have something to do with our occupation or vocation. What you do is not necessarily who you are. What you do to earn money is not always a reflection of who you are. Those who find a connection between their path and their livelihood are greatly blessed. I wholeheartedly believe that this is a state of grace available to us all. It does not, however, always come easily or in the package you might have anticipated. It often comes with great sacrifice. And sometimes we wait too long to take the journey, only to find that the journey is over.

ANOTHER WAKE-UP CALL

Two years ago, my life's path changed dramatically. Sometimes I think that just when you're settling into your life, you get a wake-up call and realize you were not really settled in at all. One morning, I received a phone call informing me that my close friend and kindred spirit, Barbara, had died. Although she had been ill, I was not prepared for her death. I didn't even get to say good-bye to her. Barbara had been the best friend you could ever hope for. Her life touched me deeply, and her death changed my life immeasurably.

For months before Barbara's death, my own health had not been very good. The long-term effects of stress and fatigue had worn me down. I knew I was fighting a battle I could not win. Just two years earlier, I had told Barbara that her business was killing her and that she needed to change her life. She was beginning to fade, and I saw it. She cried when I told her this and said that she felt trapped and afraid. She was paralyzed by financial fear and did not know how she would survive if she gave up her business. I advised her to have faith and trust that everything would work out. All the signs indicated that she was meant to move on. I told her, "God will support your decision to make this change. But you must find the courage and faith within to take the first step and let go. Holding on no longer serves you." Together we worked on finding a way to change her life's direction. Eventually she agreed to put her business and her home up for sale. Although she was afraid and did not know what her future held, she knew she could not continue her life as it was.

Unfortunately, almost two years had passed before Barbara was able to free herself of her financial burdens. Shortly thereafter, she was diagnosed with leukemia. Now, two years later, I was beginning to see the same signs in my own reflection in the mirror. I had known for a long time that I needed to make a change. I knew I needed to write. I also knew that we only get so many chances to follow our path and do the work we were brought here to do. I could feel Barbara's spirit: She was my messenger. I knew that I needed to let go of the life I was leading and my business to change my life's course. I had put off living the life I really wanted for too long.

One morning I woke up and said, "I'm selling my business and I'm going to write my book. I've been doing my work and helping other people to live their dreams, and now it is time that I do the same for myself." In other words, it was time to walk my talk. It wasn't that I didn't like what I was doing. To the contrary, I enjoyed being a financial consultant, and I was good at it. However, I knew there was a deeper purpose to my work that I had been putting off discovering. I was waiting until I had more money and more time, until my daughter was older...all excuses that stemmed from a lack of faith. Intuitively, I knew that I was meant to take this leap of faith. I could no longer delay making this choice.

Exactly one month later, I sold my business and began writing this book. I surrendered to my faith completely, and my faith was rewarded. In the months that followed, all the doors opened, and my life became flooded with miracles. My every prayer was answered. I asked for help and received it beyond my greatest hope. Friends and strangers offered their guidance and support. Before I knew it, I had an agent. All the money I needed to facilitate my decision came to me more easily than ever. In less than one year, I signed my first book contract. Shortly thereafter the publisher I had envisioned publishing this book bought it. There are no accidents or coincidences. When you are on your true path, the universe conspires and collaborates with you in the most magical way. People have told me many times how my story is the exception and not the rule. I choose to see it differently. I think that miracles are happening all the time, all around us. They are simply waiting for us to become available to them. All we need to do is step into them with faith and surrender.

When you can freely express the gift of who you are, you are in direct connection with Spirit. For here you have access to your higher self, the part of you that holds the key to manifesting your highest dreams. In this place, the possibilities are truly infinite.

EXERCISE

Your Life Path

To determine where you are in relationship to your true path, answer the following questions:

1. Do you feel you are on the right path?
2. If not, do you think you know what that path is?
3. What gifts or special talents do you have?
4. What brings you joy?
5. What aspect of you brings the most joy to others?
6. Is there something you have always wanted to do that you have yet to choose for yourself?
7. What would that be?
8. Why aren't you doing it?

When you have finished answering these questions, take time to check in with yourself, internally, and experience any emotions you might be feeling. What did the previous exercise bring up for you? What feelings of pain, loss, or grief did you experience? It is important to acknowledge and work through these feelings. Write them down in your journal while they are still fresh in your emotional body. This process will help you release and heal any residual pain and clear the way for the creative flow to come into your life.

Chapter 8

THE ALCHEMY OF FAITH

Faith — is the Pierless Bridge
Supporting what We See
Unto the Scene that We do not —

— Emily Dickinson, Poem 915, 1864

*I*n my work, I have learned that the most essential ingredient of financial well-being is faith. Without faith people often lack the confidence and trust necessary to manifest a greater reality. I believe that some people are born into their faith. It arrived with them when they entered this world and is as much a part of them as the beating of their heart. Those born with such faith seldom, if ever, question it. The destiny of many born into faith is the calling of the ministry in some form. Others nurture the faith of those around them in less obvious ways. Perhaps they are human angels, the guardians of faith and hope on earth. However, they are a relatively small proportion of the population, with the rest of us left to define, and redefine, our faith, largely in relationship to our experience. We often move in and out of our faith as it serves us, or so it often seems. It is easy to have faith when all goes well in our lives. It is an altogether different story when our lives are not moving in the direction we would like. Too often it is precisely when we need our faith the most that we abandon it or feel abandoned by it, and we lose touch with the Spirit in our daily lives.

It is easy to become disconnected from what we never completely trusted in the first place. Faith has become just another commodity that comes and goes. It seldom lasts, because life is often unfair, painful, and contradictory beyond reason. To be fully alive takes a lot of courage. Just getting out of bed some days takes more strength than we can muster. To do so every day purely on faith is an act few can commit to unconditionally.

In my own life, even as a small child, I had a spiritual calling and need to understand and know who and what God was. I went searching for God inside religion. Since there was no religion or evidence of God in my own home, I thought maybe God was in someone else's house. I remember vividly going to each of my friend's homes on my block and asking them about their God. I wanted to know what religion they belonged to, I asked to go to church with them, I read their Bibles. I was only seven, and I was on a mission. I longed to find what I knew was missing from my life. I went to many fundamentalist Christian, Catholic, Protestant, Jehovah's Witnesses, and Latter-Day Saints churches. You name it, I explored it. It was quite an education. I did not, however, find God. I did not connect with any of these religions. In any case, my mother put an end to my mission when one parent reported that when she had asked me where I came from, which I took to mean in the "original" sense, I told her that I was born in a pineapple in Hawaii. My mother was not amused. Still in the throes of my own discovery, I had needed to make up an answer. Although my mission was postponed, I secretly probed everywhere, reading everything I could, only to announce rather sadly at the age of fourteen that there was no God. It took many years and a great deal of courage to find my faith.

THE PATH OF FORGIVENESS

It was not until I was in my mid-twenties that I began to experience the presence of Spirit in my life. The first specific experience I had was profound. I had gone through a series of betrayals in my life and was feeling alone, angry, and in pain. Nothing in my life seemed to be working. One morning I woke up to the sound of a voice in my room. The voice spoke to me clearly and simply said, "It is time to forgive them."

I knew this was the truth. I knew that I could not be free until I could forgive. Those who had betrayed me had proved to be worthy opponents, the kind that you realize have the most to teach you about who you really are. It is truly amazing how a few simple words could open a door that changed my life forever. Interestingly enough, I did not have to seek out those I needed to forgive. Over the next few months, I was unexpectedly presented with an opportunity to encounter each of them. And with each encounter, each act of love and forgiveness, I became more free, and so did they.

Those who had betrayed me had needed to receive

my forgiveness as much as I had needed to forgive them. This experience was quite beautiful and affirming. I felt so alive and happy once this task of forgiveness was completed. As I began to open up again, new people and opportunities began to present themselves to me. First, I met a wonderful man who taught me to love again. He saw my ability and encouraged me to apply for a position with the 1984 Olympic Games. I was chosen for the position, and became one of the coordinators of the Olympic Torch Relay, making more money than I had ever made. It was a once-in-a-lifetime experience that allowed me to travel throughout the United States. I became friends with some of the most amazing people I have ever known. It was a time of miracles. I saw all that I received as presents from God, with whom I had successfully completed my first collaboration. It was the first in a lifetime of many. Forgiveness opens the door to receiving your divine inheritance. If you are harboring resentment and blame, you have closed the door between you and true prosperity.

In *The Notebook,* Elbert Hubburd wrote: "The ineffable joy of forgiving and being forgiven forms an ecstasy that might well arouse the envy of the gods." He is right. When you forgive, the Spirit within you wakes up and allows you to be free and available to the possibilities waiting for you to open the door of forgiveness. In working with my clients, I have found that those who were willing to forgive experience a higher degree of abundance and prosperity. Conversely, those who were unwilling to forgive themselves or others seldom moved beyond their archetypal pattern.

One of my clients, Sue, was in a twelve-step program

and had been doing her spiritual work for years. She was a kind and generous person, but the Victim type was highly active in her financial life. In spite of all the work she had done, she still clung to her "look what they've done to me" story. In her mind, her money woes were the result of terrible acts of injustice perpetrated by others, and that's where her story ended. She could see no other possibility. I told her that it was up to her to undo the past by forgiving all those she perceived had harmed her. However, she could not let go of the hurt and surrender into forgiveness. She did not understand that her unwillingness to forgive only served to hold her hostage to the past. I stopped working with her, because I knew I could not help her since she was unwilling to help herself. It was not until she became homeless and was almost stripped of everything that she found the courage to forgive.

Forgiveness is the most important step we must take on the path toward fulfillment. Unhealed wounds, resentment, and blame are obstacles that block the flow of good into our lives. It is not necessary to forgive an unjust act, just the person behind it. The act is over and complete. It cannot be changed. The only thing that can be changed is the energy between you and another human being. Freeing up this energy creates more room for you to manifest your highest good. Ask yourself these questions:

1. Who or what have you yet to forgive?
2. What is stopping you?
3. Who does this hurt most?
4. Who will be served most by your forgiveness?
5. Are you willing to release this energy from your life?

THE POWER OF PRAYER

Even though I felt a connection to God and knew that Spirit worked through me, it took years for me to develop what I now know to be my faith. I fell down a lot along the way. During one very difficult period of my life, I sought comfort in prayer. It was the first time I had prayed since I was a child. Through prayer I managed to find my way out of the darkness. The seeds of faith had been planted, and they grew quietly within, and the faith that I have cultivated since will sustain me forever. I have learned that prayer is the best way to cultivate our faith. Learning to cultivate and develop faith has also become an integral part of Money Therapy. Where I had once known that on "occasion" Spirit was at work in my life, I now know that it is always so.

Prayer is the act of being present with God, however you define that presence. It is how we actively participate and collaborate with Spirit. We can always rely on Spirit to be there for us unconditionally. We are all God's children, but unlike the parents we were born to, God has no expectations of us. God simply loves us and wants us to follow our hearts and our path and to be happy. When we stand in our own truth, we are one with God. Whatever that truth is, if we can learn to hear its voice and follow it, God is with us, holding our hand. No matter where you are in your life, how large the obstacle, how great the fear or pain, faith and prayer are the easiest way to the other side. Find the Spirit within. It may truly be the road less traveled, so take it. We have traveled the other roads only to end up taking wrong turns, missing signs along the way, or going absolutely no where at all. This is the one road we can each travel in our own way and trust we that will never be alone or lost.

Prayer As Spiritual Practice

Prayer is the most powerful tool available to us, and yet one that too few of us understand or use. Many of my clients have a difficult time praying. They are always asking me how to do it. It began to occur to me that because of our disconnectedness from Spirit, we have actually developed a discomfort with prayer and God. Many people feel they are unworthy of God's presence and that they lack the proper skills to communicate with Spirit. In truth, we all know on a soul level how to talk to God; we have simply lost touch with that dimension of ourselves or have forgotten it. Like any language we cease to actively use, we forget it. Remembering it is simply a matter of practice.

There is no one right way to pray. Prayer is a deeply personal, individual process. It does not matter how you pray, only that you pray, and that you do so frequently. You will feel and see a difference in your life directly in proportion to how often you pray. Praying daily is the best way to nourish your soul, your life, and your relationship to Spirit. It is the greatest service one can offer to the self.

Prayer is not about being small or powerless. I often encounter people who have great resistance to prayer, only to discover that this discomfort had very little to do with prayer itself. In many cases, our resistance to prayer stems from how small, helpless, and powerless we felt as children. So many of us were wounded in our primary relationships that we developed great blocks to prevent us from ever being that vulnerable again. I see this dynamic more frequently in those who were wounded in some way by their father. How hard we had to work to get the love we needed. We never stop needing that love. But we've become quite skilled at hiding that we need it and at sabotaging our ability to receive it. On some subconscious level, resistance to prayer is a fear of vulnerability and of not being loved and accepted by God. We fear that we are not worthy. But we are. We are all loved unconditionally by God. It is perhaps the only real unconditional love there is. We need only open the door to receive it.

ASKING FOR GUIDANCE

To be in the presence of God is to be both humble and powerful in the light of Spirit. Prayer is not about begging, as many people think, but about gratitude and asking for guidance. A good friend came to visit me recently and told me he was terribly frightened and in need of my advice. He did not know any longer what he was going to do with his life. He could not physically handle the work he was trained for, and he felt he had no other skills. I asked him what he thought he needed. He said, "I need cash, I just need cash." I asked him how much cash he thought he needed, how much would be enough to make him feel safe and solve his problems. He paused and said, "Well, I think $100,000 would do the job. But I don't know how to get it."

I then asked him to think about what was missing from his life now that he thought having the money would help him change. He said, "Well, I have everything I need, more than enough of some things. Nothing is really missing, except I want to be with my mother. She is old and needs my help. I cannot help her there (she lives in Europe), and I cannot bring her here. I'm trapped."

I told him he needed to follow his heart. If he needed to be with his mother, he should go to her. Waiting for the money to show up before he could be comfortable making a decision was not the answer. It never is. My friend had enough money to live in Europe for a while. And who knows what would show up for him once he got there. He began to get angry with me. My words were not what he wanted to hear. He wanted me to give him "financial advice." I told him he did not need financial advice. He had enough money. My friend admittedly had everything he needed, although he was not rich by any means. What he lacked was faith. He could not trust that if he followed his heart he would be okay. The only solution to his problem, in his mind, was money.

I asked my friend to consider praying and asking for help and guidance. Perhaps through prayer another solution would become evident. He had nothing to lose. I could not make $100,000 appear for him any more than he could. Even if I could, the money was not what he needed. He needed to cultivate his faith. He needed to connect to Spirit. In doing so, he would not only find the answer, but he would also uncover his ability to act from his heart without worrying about the size of his bank account. He was cut off from his power source, his Spirit, and this state rendered him powerless. He believed, as many of us do, that money would give him the power he needed and did not have. Before my friend left that day he thanked me and told me he knew I was right but that he just couldn't do what I said. If he only knew that by cultivating the power within him through Spirit he could do anything. If only he knew that the source of all creativity, in which all things are possible and where miracles are born, exists within each of us. If we could learn how to tap into this source, we could all truly be rich.

Reconnecting with Your Spiritual Self

In the material world in which we live, we spend so much of our life's energy trying to acquire more than what we have, wishing to be someone else, or wanting to be someplace other than where we are. These desires prevent us from experiencing the gifts that are present within us. I believe that a great part of our growing sense of dis-satisfaction and dis-illusionment stems directly from our dis-connection from Spirit. We can heal these parts of ourselves through cultivating our faith and reconnecting to our spiritual selves. To collect the disenfranchised parts of who we are, we must re-member the Spirit from which we came. We have been so caught up in living purely in one dimension of our lives, that we have neglected the other dimensions entirely, including our souls and our greatest resource, God.

We did not just arrive here to work, acquire, and shop. We are spiritual beings born into human bodies, sent here with a path and a purpose. We have simply become so disconnected from the knowledge and essence of who we are that we can no longer consciously remember or relate to anything that is not visible, that does not exist in this dimension. That does not mean these things aren't there. They are. They always were. They will be long after we are gone. The greatest tragedy one could possibly suffer in this life is to have come and gone without having known the beauty and power of faith in one's existence. It is faith, this connection to Spirit, that is meant to serve and guide us while we are here. Faith is our greatest gift, and we cannot properly receive it without cultivating our relationship to it. This has been my greatest lesson. It is what I needed to learn, so that I might teach and offer this gift to others. Metaphorically, I often see the early stages of Money Therapy as the road leading to the door of a new way of being and seeing. Cultivating faith, one of the final stages of Money Therapy, is the key to opening the door and keeping it open.

In cultivating faith, you must step back and look at what you believe and how that belief was instilled in you. So much of what we believe is nothing more than someone else's beliefs or our reaction to them. We took ownership of these beliefs unconsciously. Therefore, we must look inside the box of our beliefs, pulling out each of them one by one and reexamining them. I like to use the visual image of a box, because doing so allows us to separate our beliefs from who we are. A belief has its own energy, and you can choose to own or discard it as it serves you. For example, here are a few beliefs that have been passed down unconsciously through our language:

> Money is the root of all evil. (This is actually a misquote from the Bible, which says, "The love of money is the root of all evil.")
> Money is dirty.
> As a result, people with lots of money are filthy rich.
> Money and greed are married to each other.
> The rich get richer; the poor get poorer.
> You can never be too rich or too thin.
> Only the poor know humility.
> I can't afford it.
> I'm broke.

Exercise

Your Belief Box

Bring out your box. Many of my clients make or buy a special box just for this purpose. Then ask yourself these questions, and write your answers in your journal.

1. What do I truly believe about money?
2. How did I develop these beliefs?
3. Which of these beliefs do I consciously practice? Does what I practice "mirror" my relationship with money?
4. Which of these beliefs no longer serve me? (Write them down on another sheet of paper.)
5. Am I willing to let go of what no longer serves me?
6. If your answer is yes, tear up the list from question four. Consciously release these beliefs. You have no ownership of them. They are no longer a part of your conscious reality. It is your choice.
7. You are free to choose and rechoose new beliefs. What beliefs from list one and three do you wish to continue to choose? What new beliefs do you desire to bring into your life? Write them down.

Put this last list back in the box. Whether you use a tangible box or one you keep in your mind, it is important to periodically visit and reexamine its contents and to repeat the above exercise, discarding what no longer serves you and adding what will. Remember, spiritual practice is a journey requiring commitment of both thought and action. The more you practice, the greater the rewards and the sooner you will become a money Magician.

Chapter 9

THE MAGICIAN'S GUIDE
TO MONEY

Every man is the architect of his own fortune.

— Sallust, speech to Caesar (first century B.C.)

Magicians are masters in the art of transforming reality. To attain this level of mastery, Magicians know they must be fully conscious of their reality and that which they seek to transform. They are students of the past and teachers of the future. However, Magicians seek to live in the present moment in a state of grace and gratitude. They are followers of the light and leaders of the way. They know the source lies within, and they have access to its infinite power.

Magicians are aware of the money game, but they strive not to become entangled in it. They know that the money game is about the illusion of money as the source. Magicians are connected to the real Source, and they believe that money is an unlimited supply of creative expression provided by the Divine Spirit. Whenever money Magicians begin to experience difficulty with money or a specific financial issue comes to the forefront, they seek to resolve whatever problem within themselves is creating the circumstance. The Magician knows that any feeling of constriction about money will block the way of its creative flow. Therefore, a Magician strives to maintain a high level of consciousness and actively seeks to understand and remove any fear or obstacle in their path. Magicians know they must maintain an open and conscious relationship with money. They recognize that money is but one of many resources available to meet their needs. These types trust in their ability to manifest the money they need to fulfill their life's path and purpose. They know and live the abundant life. The Magician does not seek prosperity for its own sake; rather, she trusts that if prosperity serves her path, it will be received. Whatever the Magician needs in the material world will be provided. The Magician works on the intentional manifestation of what serves his higher purpose and spiritual path.

THE APPRENTICE MAGICIAN'S GUIDE

Wherever you are on your path at this time, whatever money type and issues are present in your life, it is essential that you identify and work through them so that you can manifest the relationship with money that you desire. Realize that while abundance is available and easily accessible to everyone, prosperity, if it does not serve your path, may not be part of your future. However, you can trust that you will always have enough. When you surrender this to Spirit, the weight of your financial struggles will be lighter, for you will no longer be carrying it alone.

Becoming a money Magician is a process, a pilgrimage, that consists of the following steps:

1. Understanding how you play the money game and the places where you get caught in the money trap.

2. Taking a close look at your personal and ancestral history with money and understanding how it may have imposed certain patterns and beliefs that do not serve you on your path.

3. Becoming intimately familiar with the money type that is active in your life. This involves making a commitment to understanding and changing your conscious behavior so that you can create a healthier relationship with money.

4. Redefining your true worth and seeing the value of your life in relationship to who you are and the gifts you have to offer. You are infinitely more valuable than the amount of money you have or do not have. The truth of who you are is not about money.

5. Establishing a new foundation and relationship with money based on how you desire money to show up for you and what you truly need money to provide for you.

6. Becoming conscious of your thoughts, language, and actions in relationship to money. What you think, say, and do has a powerful

effect on your ability to transform and manifest your reality. Consciously choose the position of loving-kindness so that you can be in alignment with your true power and that of the Source. It is also important that you work quickly to remove feelings of fear and control from your conscious mind and actions.

7. Seeking to know and to follow the direction of your path and purpose. When you do this, you will never be without. Abundance is your divine inheritance. Those who seek the kingdom from within will always have access to the outer kingdom and all that it offers.

8. Doing your spiritual work every day of your life. Pray, meditate, connect to Spirit in whatever way works for you and as frequently as you can. You will see your life change in direct proportion to the time and energy you are willing to pay homage to your soul and connect to the Spirit within.

9. Cultivating your faith. Carry it with you always and trust that all your needs will be met. When you can build this trust, you will never feel lost or abandoned.

10. Carrying with you always the powerful elixir of truth and love, the most transformative ingredients in the world today and forever.

Magicians are gifted alchemists who practice the art of manifestation through spiritual transformation. The simple formula below is the Magician's guide to prosperity.

The Magician's Formula for Prosperity Consciousness

M = Masters in the art of transforming reality
A = Aligned with the Universal Spiritual Principles
G = Guided by insight and revelation
I = Integrity-based in all actions
C = Connected to the Source
I = Intuitive
A = Abundant
N = Not attached to outcome

The Magician's Guide to Manifesting Money

Here are nine guidelines to follow you on the path to becoming a money Magician. Embrace and integrate each one into your life and you, too, will be able to manifest all that you need.

1. Seek first to build the portfolio of your life. Before you begin to think about manifesting prosperity in your life, you must know your reason for seeking it. What life are you seeking? Begin to build that life day by day, brick by brick. Lay the foundation for the life you want now. Do not wait to have money before you begin.

2. Ask yourself what you want money to transform in your life. You must know the answer to this question before you can expect to manifest it. The more specific you are, the greater success you will have.

3. Seek the kingdom within first. The secret to

happiness and success should be based on your internal needs and desires. Work to create a world that reflects who you are.

4. Make certain the reality you seek to transform is in alignment with the spiritual truths to which you ascribe.

5. Let yourself be guided by insight and revelation. Develop your intuition about money so that you will know where to focus your intention. Avoid putting time, energy, or money into areas of your life that take you off your path.

6. Resolve to make decisions with integrity and to act with integrity around money. Only you know your own truth: Follow that guidance.

7. Ask for what you want and need specifically. Pray for and meditate on receiving all that the Divine Spirit has intended for you.

8. Remain detached from outcome. Trust that you will receive all that you need that serve your highest good and your life's purpose. Magicians know that attachment is the root of all unhappiness and disappointment.

9. Nurture your soul and stay connected to Spirit. Stay plugged into this great power Source, and let it guide you on your path.

CHARTING YOUR COURSE

We constantly hear about how important it is to have a good "financial plan," which consists of taking a picture of where you are now (including your income, assets, and liabilities) and then projecting into the future where you will most likely be, all factors considered.

The results of a financial plan indicate how close you

are to meeting your financial goals and objectives and offers advice on how to better achieve your desired financial outcome. Financial planning is a very valuable tool, because it not only provides financial perspective, but it also increases your consciousness about the dynamics of money. As a financial advisor, I certainly advocate financial planning. But, unfortunately, financial planners and investment advisors seldom look at the inner life of a person in relationship to creating their financial plan. Traditional planning looks purely at the outer manifestation of people's lives. Even the most sophisticated financial plan in the world will provide little if any assistance unless it mirrors your innermost dreams and desires. A successful financial plan begins on the inside and works its way out into the material world. Money Magicians know that the key to true happiness and success lies in their ability to transform their inner world into physical form in the material world.

The Pyramid of Financial Planning (Outer Consciousness)

The pyramid of financial planning has been used in the financial world for many years. It has served as a visual aid to help people understand the importance of building a financial future from a strong foundation and then proceeding in a safe, progressive manner. A typical financial planning pyramid appears on page 142.

Traditionally, the key to a successful plan is to start with a strong foundation and move up the pyramid over time. For example, if you were to simply start at the top, with speculative investing (which is what the Fool money type would be most likely to do), you could easily suffer a financial setback that could take years to

Pyramid of Financial Planning
(Outer Consciousness)

Fifth
tier =
Speculative
investments
such as options,
IPOs, oil and
gas, and limited
partnerships

Fourth tier = Retirement
assets such as IRAs, 401(k)s,
and pension plans

Third tier = Investments
such as stocks, bonds, and
mutual funds

Second tier = Tangible assets such as
home, real estate, and land

Foundation = Safety net
(consists of liquid cash, insurance, and
equivalents)

recover from. However, by adding money to each of the categories over time, theoretically you would cover all the bases and create a balanced financial life. The goal is to have a balanced portfolio supported by a strong foundation. This prevents an unexpected turn in the market, a life event, or a crisis from destroying everything you've worked to build.

BUILDING THE PYRAMID OF YOUR LIFE

Just as the pyramid of financial planning helps you to achieve your financial goals, your life pyramid helps you to establish a foundation for your internal goals. This life pyramid helps you to stay on track with what really matters to you. It is not up to a financial advisor to tell you what is important to you. This is your life; it's your job to figure out what really matters to you and how to use your gifts. This part of your plan should serve as a litmus test for determining if what you're creating in the material world is a true reflection of innermost dreams and desires. It will also help you avoid getting caught in an unnecessary money trap.

A client of mine, an Innocent who is well on her way to becoming a money Magician, called me recently and said, "I'm thinking of buying a house in Palm Springs. A friend and I were talking, and we think we could afford to buy one if we pooled our money. What do you think of that idea?" My inner voice told me she was moving off focus. She was making great progress, but her tendency to be impulsive was surfacing. I asked her why she wanted to buy a house in Palm Springs. She responded, "Well, I don't think I can ever afford to own a home in Los Angeles, and I've always liked the desert, and it's much more affordable. At least I'll have something when I retire."

I told her that while all her reasons were legitimate, I sensed they were driven by fear and feelings of lack and limitation. She answered, "Well, I guess I need to remove the thoughts about not being able to have what I want here."

I added, "Maybe you need to think about why you believe you can't have it on your own. Haven't you manifested everything you've needed so far?"

She agreed that she had, so I asked her to spend some time determining if a house in Palm Springs was what she really needed and if shifting her focus at this point in her work would serve her on her path. Her life as an artist was really beginning to take off. Diverting time, energy, and money from her path for something based on her fear of not having a place to live twenty years from now might sabotage the reality she was trying to manifest today. She was still working on her foundation.

Remain conscious of the motivations behind your decisions and stay focused on what you really want. A sudden move in the wrong direction, especially if it is based on fear, will only be a detour from your goal. All money Magicians are very intentional about their choices and how they use their resources.

The Magician's Prosperity Pyramid (Inner Consciousness)

Creating a prosperity pyramid will help you clarify your inner consciousness so that you may rely on it as your guiding strength. Remember, a Magician seeks the kingdom within as the first step. With this knowledge, you will possess the power to transform the outer world.

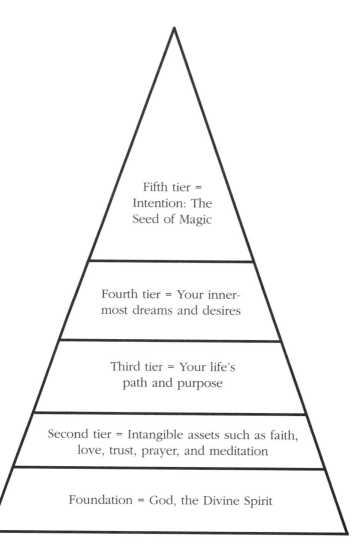

The Magician's Prosperity Pyramid
(Inner Consciousness)

Fifth tier =
Intention: The
Seed of Magic

Fourth tier = Your inner-
most dreams and desires

Third tier = Your life's
path and purpose

Second tier = Intangible assets such as faith,
love, trust, prayer, and meditation

Foundation = God, the Divine Spirit

Create Your Own Prosperity Pyramid

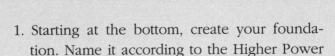

1. Starting at the bottom, create your foundation. Name it according to the Higher Power you believe in.
2. On the next tier, add all the intangible assets you possess and are committed to.
3. What do you believe to be your path and purpose? If you do not know, make a commitment to discovering it.
4. What are your innermost dreams and desires? These can be tangible or intangible.
5. State your intention. What is the reality you seek to transform in your life?

Now, create your financial pyramid:

1. What kind of financial foundation do you have right now? Write this information inside the pyramid.
2. What tangible assets do you own (type and amount)?
3. What investments do you have (type and amount)?
4. What retirement planning assets do you have (type and amount)?

5. What speculative investments do you have (type and amount)?

Based on your financial pyramid, ask yourself:

1. How strong is your foundation?
2. How balanced is your pyramid?
3. What areas need reinforcement?

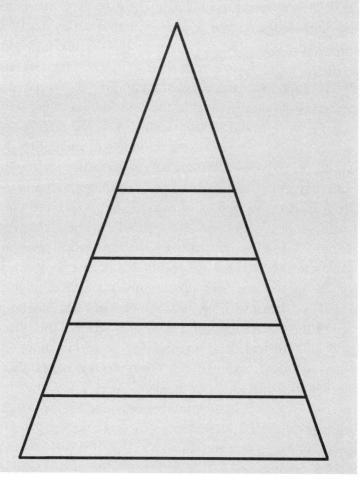

THE PILGRIMAGE OF THE MAGI

The root word for Magician is *magi*. One of the earliest references to the word *magi* is the biblical reference of the Three Wise Men. The magi were guided by the light of a star in the Far East, which led them on a pilgrimage to Israel to pay homage to the newborn King, the Son of God. Each one brought with them a different gift: gold, frankincense, and myrrh. The Three Wise Men were also referred to as kings, because they possessed the knowledge of the kingdom within. They had followed the light that led them to the Source and paid homage to the Source with their gifts. Each possessed a different gift and had traveled far to give it. No gift was perceived as more valuable than the others. They were equally represented before God.

This story serves as a wonderful metaphor for would-be Magicians. We are all on a journey. While the path may not be clearly marked, if we have faith and ask for guidance, we will be shown the way. Like the three magi, money Magicians are guided by the light from within. This light is available to everyone whose eyes are willing to see beyond the visible. Magicians do not wait for the money to show up to embark on their pilgrimage. They travel with the gifts they have. They pay homage to the Source by using their gifts wisely. They have faith and trust in their divine inheritance, not knowing when or how it will manifest. They do not worry about the details, for that is not their job. They know they are capable of manifesting whatever they need to help them fulfill their path and purpose. To this end, they know they will be given everything.

For many years, I struggled with why I never seemed

to "get ahead" financially. I had always worked very hard and taken more risks than most people. It somehow seemed unfair to me that I wasn't more financially successful, given my efforts. Sure, I made a very good living, but I still felt somewhat cheated that I wasn't "rich."

Then one day it hit me that I had not been seeing my life correctly. I have always valued my personal freedom and independence above everything. Also, my home environment is essential to my sense of peace and well-being. As I began to do an accounting of my life, I realized how everything had worked in the most synchronistic way to create the life that I most valued. I have been self-employed most of my life. I have been completely financially independent since I was seventeen years old. I have traveled extensively. I have lived in some of the most wonderful places on the Earth. Each time I have moved, my family and friends come to visit and say, "How do you keep finding these wonderful places?" My answer has always been, "I just keep asking for what I need."

I am a money Magician. I know how to create and manifest everything I need, including money, to support my path and the life I have chosen. I have enough of everything. I am as "rich" and prosperous as anyone I know. Another important realization about money that I have had is this: Having too much money too soon often takes people off their path. For instance, I know that if I had made a "fortune" early in my life, I most likely would not have stayed on this path. I would not have endured the hardships I have known or learned the lessons that were necessary to bring me to this point. The consequences of moving off my path would have been immeasurable, for I would not have met the people I have known or had the opportunity to do this work or to make a difference in people's lives, however large or small. And chances are, I would not be writing this book.

When I graduated from college as an English major, I remember saying that I had given up the idea of being a writer and a teacher because I was tired of being poor. I was too familiar with that experience, and I was ready to be prosperous. Well, twenty years have passed and this year I will be attending my college reunion. I will be showing up, full circle, as writer, teacher, and financial advisor. It was my path all along.

Listen to the Spirit within. You too will be guided to take the path that you were meant to travel. It may not always be easy, but everything will turn out as it should. You will know what it is to live in abundance. You may even experience tremendous prosperity. So let go, and do not be afraid. Risk everything if you have to. Trust that you will be taken care of, and you will be. The road to becoming a Magician begins with the first step. Whoever and wherever you are right now...open the door and begin your journey. Everything you need is available to you. If you know the way, follow it. If you don't know, ask for directions. Ask and you shall receive.

Chapter 10

WHERE DO WE GO FROM HERE?

*The aim of life is to live, and to live means to be aware, joy-
ously, drunkenly, serenely, divinely aware.*

— Henry Miller, *The Wisdom of the Heart,* 1941

*T*he most important asset you will ever possess is
the life you were given. What you choose to do
with this gift in the relatively short period of time you have
possession of it will determine whether or not you leave
this world as wealthy as you came in. For you were given
all you ever needed in the seed of possibility that was
born as you. You are a miracle. Anyone, including you,
who tells you differently is wrong. Remember the truth,
and live your life surrounded by this knowledge. Form a
circle of belief around yourself that says: "I am a miracle
and the seed of infinite possibility was born within me and
is with me still." Do not let anyone or anything that happens to you alter this belief, for it is an eternal truth.

On the morning that I began writing the conclusion

to this book, my inner guide said, "Pay attention to the landscape of your life." So I wandered outside and was drawn to a magnificent old tree in my front yard that I often sit with and observe. This old pine possesses a majesty and wisdom that I have always found comforting. Nature is such a powerful teacher. As I meditated on the tree, I began thinking about how long ago this tree began its journey from a seed. It must be more than two hundred years old. It has such a simple life. It does not have to do or think about anything to be beautiful. It does not have to process change, for its changes occur naturally. It does not have to be conscious or make choices. The tree does not have to do anything. It just is. What began as a seed grew almost effortlessly to tremendous heights. It has expanded in many ways, in both depth and height and has many branches that extend and lift up to the sky. It has gone through many seasons and changes during its long life, all because of one tiny seed that was planted long ago. The tree has a purpose that it simply lives every day.

God is the most magnificent artist. Every living thing you see existed first in the imagination of the Divine Spirit. Everything in nature was beautifully painted and crafted into form with intention and purpose. Of course, the difference between us and the tree is that we were given the power of creative thought and free will. These are the gifts that make us human. We were given life, a blank canvas, and an imagination of our own to paint and create our own reality. Unlike the tree, whose entire reality was born of a single seed, we must use the gifts we've been given — creativity, imagination, consciousness, and free will — to grow into the fullness of our being. We must grow the seed of our potential by working the soil of our life daily. When we forget to do this, we are wasting the wealth hidden in our potential.

Think about it. If every day, not just some day (which is an illusion anyway), you planted a seed for change, growth, and transformation in your life, imagine how the tree of your life could grow? Nature does not have a consciousness and the ability to create itself. We alone were given this gift. We cannot afford to just sit around and be unconscious of who we are and what we are doing. To do this is to live in stagnation, which in nature is the beginning stage of death. Nature is a mirror and a metaphor for our lives, a subject to reflect on. "Pay attention to the landscape of your life," the inner voice said. What part of your life has been dormant for too long? Pay attention to the places within you that are stagnant. They are blocks to the flow of the abundance that awaits you.

PLANTING THE SEEDS

So where do you go from here? Look closely at where you are right now in your life. Find the places within that need to grow and change, and plant a seed for that change today. If you want more love in your life, plant a seed and become the love you want. That way you'll always have enough. If you're waiting for the right partner, plant a seed and practice being the perfect partner to yourself. Doing this will help you to give first what you desire most to receive. If you want more money, plant a seed to change your relationship with money. Be conscious of your intentions, and seek to understand the questions before you go looking for the answers. The answers and the way will be shown to you.

Whatever you want to change in this life, you must be willing to be there first and perhaps to do things differently. You cannot ask for circumstances alone to change while you sit passively back and wait for the results. This is your life: No one can do the work for you. You are the artist, so make your life a work of art. This is no easy task, but it is always worth the effort. Have you ever watched a seed work its tiny self up from the ground? No matter how hard and resistant the ground above it is, the seed still manages to push through. This is an amazing and miraculous process. So is your life. Whatever you need to push through to get to the other side, you can do it. These are not just words. I, too, have known hardship and adversity. They are real. I also know that it is through struggle that we learn to know our strengths and discover our courage. Do not believe for a minute that you are alone in this process. You are not. You still have much to give and to receive. The fact that you are here is the only proof you need. If your work was done, you wouldn't be reading this book. It is that simple. You can begin by consciously planting at least one seed every day of your life: a seed for change, creativity, love, joy, abundance, or prosperity. See what you can become. You are the gardener of your life. Love and nurture it. Believe in its possibility. God will provide the warmth, the sun, and the Light. Work it daily. Start today.

SIXTY-DAY PROSPERITY PROGRAM

It is said that old habits die hard and new ones are not born easily in their place. To use the information you have received in this book, you need to begin making conscious choices to change your life and relationship with money while the information is still fresh in your mind. If you only read this book but do nothing to change your thoughts and actions, you will have missed an opportunity to change your life. I recommend that, to successfully implement any meaningful change, particularly one that involves lifelong unconscious behavior, you dedicate a minimum of sixty days to creating a new consciousness.

Within the first thirty days, you should begin to see a difference in your level of awareness, and you may even experience a distinct shift in your financial life. However, do not discontinue the program before the end of the sixty-day period, because your mind is likely to revert back to its previous patterns. Studies indicate that patterns of behavior become physically formed in the brain over time. Until new behaviors are firmly established, your mind is naturally inclined to resume old patterns. Consequently, the longer you repeat any positive thought or behavior, the more likely it will stick and become an automatic response.

CREATING YOUR PROSPERITY PROGRAM

1. Create a list of everything you are grateful for.
2. Create a list of everything you need money for that you do not already have.
3. Create a sacred altar in your home consisting of anything that represents what you value most in life and what you seek to manifest. (If you don't have these things, create a collage with pictures that represent them.) Place a candle on your altar.

4. Spend a minimum of five minutes in the morning and five minutes at night before your altar
in prayer and meditation. Begin by lighting the
candle as a symbol of the Light from within
that connects you to Spirit. Read aloud from
your gratitude list and give thanks for what
you have been given. Read aloud from your
list of money needs and ask that you be
shown the way to receiving all that you need.
The power of invocation has been used effec-
tively for centuries. As you develop your relationship with Spirit, you will learn the dance of
collaboration.

5. Keep a small tablet with you at all times.
Whenever you think or say anything negative
about money, whether it is a passing fear or a
thought about yourself or someone else, write
it down. Catch yourself the minute you say or
think anything that contradicts your intention.
As you write it down, consciously say to yourself, "This is not what I truly believe, nor does
this belief serve my purpose. I will not house
this thought in my mind any longer."

6. Try to avoid people who have negative money
attitudes and behavior. Their energy is coun-
terproductive to making the changes you are
trying to create in your life. If it is not possible
to avoid them, try asking them not to express
their negative thoughts to you.

7. Keep a one hundred dollar bill in your wallet
or purse as a reminder of the invisible supply.
Try not to spend it. There is more where it

came from. This money is but a symbol of all that is available to you. Just because you don't have all the money you feel you need at this moment does not mean it isn't there. There is an invisible supply of money, and all that you need has been earmarked for you.

8. Practice being generous through acts of conscious giving. Pay attention to the unspoken needs of those you love and those of others. Do they need something that you have to give? A kind word, a gesture, a smile, a meal… it does not matter what it is. What matters is that you practice knowing and living from a place of abundance.

9. Choose a sacred witness to share this experience with. Choose someone you trust with your life and with whom you can share everything and know that you are safe. Ask them to hold the space for you to make your dreams a reality. Only discuss what you are doing with this one person during this time.

10. Surrender your fears of lack and limitation. Write a letter to God (or to your friend) and send all your fear on a vacation for sixty days. Be prepared, however, for it might not come back.

11. Look in the mirror every day and remind yourself that there is more to you than what you see. You are very familiar with this outer reflection of yourself. How well do you know the inside? Take the time in the next sixty days to become more familiar with the inner you. One thing is certain: All of you is well worth knowing.

When sixty days have passed, you may or may not have manifested the money or changes you have worked to transform. That does not mean it isn't going to happen. Remember that although we must never be afraid to ask for what we want, we must remain unattached to the outcome. Ask and release. Stay focused on your path and go about your life. Leave the details to God. This is the hardest part of the lesson, but once you've mastered it, everything else will seem easy. Hold onto your faith like the arm of a fierce friend. In time, you will see changes in yourself and your life that are clear indications of what is yet to come. Along the way, you may encounter people, even friends and family, who challenge your faith and make you feel your efforts are fruitless. They are not. It takes time to become a Magician. Stay on the path and always maintain your connection to Spirit. Live your life with a full heart and do what needs to be done with faith and trust in the right outcome.

RESOURCES AND
RECOMMENDED READING

Beckwith, Michael. *40-Day Mind Fast, Soul Feast.* Culver City, Calif.: Agape Press, 2000.

Chopra, Deepak. *The Seven Spiritual Laws of Success.* San Rafael, Calif.: Amber-Allen Publishing and New World Library, 1994.

Gawain, Shatki. *Living in the Light.* Novato, Calif.: New World Library, 1998.

Harvey, Andrew. *The Direct Path: Creating a Journey to the Divine Using the World's Mystical Traditions.* New York: Broadway Books, 2000.

Holmes, Ernest. *How to Change Your Life.* Deerfield, Calif.: Science of Mind Publishing, Health Communications, 1982.

Needleman, Jacob. *Money and the Meaning of Life.* New York: Doubleday, 1991.

Rumi, Jalal Al-Din. *The Illuminated Rumi.* Translation and commentary by Coleman Barks. New York: Broadway Books, 1997.

Shield, Benjamin and Richard Carlson, eds. *For the Love of God: Handbook for the Spirit.* Novato, Calif.: New World Library, 1997.

Weatherford, Jack. *The History of Money.* New York: Three Rivers Press, 1997.

ABOUT THE AUTHOR

*D*eborah Price has been in the financial services industry for fifteen years. She has worked with firms such as Merrill Lynch, Mass Mutual, and Edward Jones Investments. She is a licensed independent investment advisor and stockbroker affiliated with Select Advisors, Inc. Currently, she works as a money coach and financial advisor. She conducts Money Therapy seminars for both individuals and corporations. She is also the author of *Start Investing Online Today* (Adams Media). Deborah lives on a vineyard in Healdsburg, California, with her daughter.

For information regarding Money Coaching or Money Therapy seminars, contact Deborah Price at (800) 639-0977 or visit her website at www.money-therapy.com.

ew World Library is dedicated to publishing books, audiocassettes, and videotapes that inspire and challenge us to improve the quality of our lives and our world.

Our books and tapes are available
in bookstores everywhere.
For a catalog of our complete library
of fine books and cassettes, contact:

New World Library
14 Pamaron Way
Novato, CA 94949

Phone: (415) 884-2100
Fax: (415) 884-2199
Or call toll-free (800) 972-6657
Catalog requests: Ext. 50
Ordering: Ext. 52

E-mail: escort@nwlib.com
http://www.newworldlibrary.com